Praise for *The ROI of LOL*

"Steve Cody understands the profound power of humor in building human connections in business. Steve's a funny guy, and he applies that talent in a purpose-driven way: to forge meaningful relationships with employees, customers, industry leaders, and others who are essential to his company's business. His humor creates stronger bonds; he never chases a laugh at others' expense. I guarantee a strong ROI if you invest the time to read this book and see the magic come to life."

—PAT FORD, professional-in-residence, University of Florida

"The geniuses of comedy! Steve Cody and Clayton Fletcher share hilarious stories and evidence-based insights of turn-key techniques—based on stand-up, improv, and sketch comedy—to demonstrate the power of and desperate need for fusing humor into the workplace to strengthen leaders and organizational outcomes. I loved the book. However, it is missing the 'Top 10 List of Funny Leaders,' of which I would expect top billing."

—TINA McCORKINDALE, chairman and CEO, the Institute for Public Relations

"Steve Cody has done a great service for workplaces by reminding us of the value that humor brings to work. It defuses tensions, enhances teamwork, and often makes new perspectives possible to hear. He'll inspire many to see work and levity in a new light."

—OSCAR SURIS, SVP, chief communications officer, Duke Energy Corporation

"Indulge in the laughter, embrace the lessons, and embark on a profound leadership transformation. Steve Cody and Clayton Fletcher have gifted us with a book that is timely, thought-provoking, and a catalyst for positive change."

—CHARLENE WHEELESS, award-winning author of *You Are Enough*

"At the heart of good communication is wit and wisdom— and at its best a good laugh. In these contentious days, a little levity can go a long way toward creating a more caring and open workplace. Steve Cody and Clayton Fletcher remind us of that fact and show us how."

—MIKE FERNANDEZ, cohost of *The Crux* podcast and senior vice president of Enbridge

THE ROI OF... LOL

HOW LAUGHTER BREAKS DOWN WALLS, DRIVES COMPELLING STORYTELLING, AND CREATES A HEALTHY WORKPLACE

STEVE CODY and CLAYTON FLETCHER

HarperCollins Leadership

AN IMPRINT OF HarperCollins

Published by HarperCollins Leadership, an imprint of HarperCollins Focus LLC.

Any internet addresses, phone numbers, or company or product information printed in this book are offered as a resource and are not intended in any way to be or to imply an endorsement by HarperCollins Leadership, nor does HarperCollins Leadership vouch for the existence, content, or services of these sites, phone numbers, companies, or products beyond the life of this book.

ISBN 978-1-4002-4376-1 (eBook)

ISBN 978-1-4002-4370-9 (TP)

Library of Congress Control Number: 2023943214

Printed in the United States of America

23 24 25 26 27 LBC 5 4 3 2 1

*To our personal and professional families
and friends, without whose support we'd still
be editing the first paragraph.*

*To all the organizations who have trusted us
to infuse comedy into their cultures and help
them overcome seemingly insurmountable
obstacles with a smile.*

*And to anyone who's ever laughed
through the madness.*

CONTENTS

Contents

FOREWORD

NOTE TO READER: Linda Rutherford and Steve Cody have known and worked together for many years. They serve on two of the PR profession's most influential industry boards, and Linda has always been ready to provide insights, case studies, and observations on any and all Peppercomm-branded research over the years. Her company is of, by, and for love and laughter. In fact, even their stock symbol on the NYSE is "LUV."

Southwest Airlines' beloved founder and chairman emeritus, Herb Kelleher, used to say that the "secret sauce" of our workplace culture is that our people (whom we call Employees, and we capitalize the "E" because they are important) take their work seriously but don't take themselves too seriously—that no one needed to shed their personality when they came to work. He took great pride in espousing the terms *love* (or LUV if you're familiar with the Southwest Airlines stock symbol) and *laughter* as key cornerstones of our culture. He used to say that Wall Street thought using those terms was heresy in corporate America—and he spent his career proving them wrong. If you look back at our airline's record of no layoffs, strong balance sheets, investment-grade credit rating, iconic corporate culture, employer brand, stock price, and so on, you will see there is a strong correlation between our commitment to love and laughter and our operational and financial excellence as a New York Stock Exchange–traded company.

It's the power of those intangibles that Steve Cody and Clayton Fletcher explore in this work: the spaces where business and humor intersect and when and why it's important. Steve's study of comedians and the comedic process nets an important insight—that comedians are, at their heart, highly effective communicators. I always marveled at Herb's ability to connect with any human being, from a US congressperson to a university janitor, and make them feel important. He had a gift to immediately engage through his wit, humor, and gift of storytelling.

I remember some years back escorting Herb to a speaking engagement at the National Press Club in Washington, DC. It was going to be a less-than-friendly audience with no "off-the-record" option. Armed with the knowledge that the attendees might be adversarial, Herb began in true Herb fashion. "Ladies and gentlemen. Thank you for having me here today. I'm not sure what qualifies me to stand up here today and be your featured speaker other than the National Press Club found my skill at projectile vomiting and ability to keep marinara sauce off my tie compelling." To say he disarmed the audience was an understatement. He had them eating out of his hand, with one softball question after another. The resulting headlines were a PR dream. Humor had both engaged and disarmed them. What CEO starts off a speech using projectile vomiting in a sentence?

Through his example, he taught that skill to our Southwest people, who have carried that mission on for more than fifty years. If you've ever been on a LUV aircraft, you might have heard the public safety announcements rapped, sung, or injected with a joke or two. Early in my career at

Southwest, I remember a complaint that was filed with our governmental regulatory agency that it was unprofessional and risky to mix humor with our preflight public safety announcements. As a result, the agency did a study—and guess what they determined? That passengers actually paid *more* attention to the safety announcements *because* they were entertaining, compelling, and funny. One of my favorites? "Did anyone drop a wallet? Everyone look to see if this is your wallet I'm holding up. . . . Okay, ladies and gentlemen, now that I have your attention, I'd like to point out the safety features of this Boeing 737." Another: "There may be fifty ways to leave your lover, but there are only six ways off this aircraft in the event of an emergency." Our flight attendants follow the rules and regulations and then use their own humor and creativity to get the job done.

Steve and Clayton will take you on their own journey, and that of their agency, to point out that there is power in humor—in business, in talent attraction, in managing a dynamic workforce, in change management, and in brand differentiation. If you're trying to create a workplace that stands out from the competition, manages through uncertainty, and is just plain *fun*—this is a great read. Dig in, learn lots, and laugh often!

Linda Rutherford

Chief administration officer
and chief communications officer,
Southwest Airlines Company

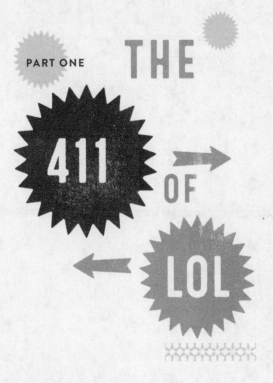

PART ONE

THE
411
OF
LOL

THE CASE *for* COMEDY AT WORK

1

INTRODUCTION

The Need for Laughter in an Uncertain World

IF YOU OPENED this book hoping to find a quick fix or an exact percentage increase in revenues that you will get from laughing at work, we suggest instead you pick up a copy of *Harry Potter Goes to Washington*. We actually don't know whether Harry's ever been to Washington, or if he's even ever left London. We've never even met him. What we do know is that the true effect of laughter in the workplace is achieved only in the long term. *The ROI of LOL* is the culmination of learning about what comedians know that businesspeople should know. It's achieved over time, much like a wizard's education at Hogwarts (see Dumbledore for more info).

Realizing the results of a comedy-infused culture is akin to building a World Series winner from a perpetual last-place laughing stock (note: the '69 Mets are a textbook example). It takes the intentional laying of a lot of groundwork and the commitment of a dedicated C-suite that really wants to become an employer of choice.

We're not giving you a shot of progesterone to increase your home run count but rather a nutrition plan that you can implement to enrich your corporate body and achieve better results in the long run. Of course, there are short-term benefits to laughing today, and we'll explore them herein, but the real return on investment here is the World Series ring that comes from infusing your workplace with a steady diet of ha ha ha. As a bonus, if you fall on hard times, you can always hock the ring for a pretty penny on eBay.

We all know how the world changed forever in March 2020. The global pandemic arrived and with it that most cringeworthy of phrases, "the new normal." Virtually overnight, the ways in which organizations viewed their responsibilities to the planet changed. So did the relationship between the company and the employee. And it's never going back to the old normal. And even as Labor Department statistics ebb and flow, and the pendulum swings from a labor advantage to a management advantage, the facts about laughter don't change. Employees care about much more than profits, and so do smart companies that want to retain them.

In the 1987 film *Wall Street*, Michael Douglas's Gordon Gekko tells his minions, "Greed is good." We see his point, but we think laughter is gooder. Regardless of how greedy the investment community is, the fact remains you'll never achieve your top- and bottom-line financial goals without a focus first on your people. Culture trumps innovation, strategy, creativity, and everything else you might think it takes to become the next big disruptor in your industry. And Clayton in particular knows a thing or two about disruptors; he's handled more hecklers than a traffic cop in Midtown Manhattan.

Steve sees himself as a medieval alchemist and has actually transformed hay into gold in his backyard. We're convinced that the workplace, while often stressful and at times as unpleasant as a tour of a Trenton sewage plant, should be healthy, and that when it is, productivity skyrockets. It seems to us we need laughter now more than ever. Moshe Waldoks, author of *The Big Book of Jewish Humor,* is quoted as saying, "A sense of humor can help you overlook the unattractive, tolerate the unpleasant, cope with the unexpected, and smile through the unbearable."

The role of comedy in the business world is evolving as we speak. Not only are we spending more time in our "home offices," we now have artificial intelligence threatening our jobs! By the way, this entire chapter was written by R2-D2. Nice job, R2. He's a hard worker, but he's useless before his second cup of espresso. Although the robots may eventually take over, one thing artificial intelligence can't do is read a room. The robots may be able to respond to text, but they will never be able to deal with a stag party heckler in a comedy club or to *sense* whether or not the client is buying what you're selling. Being in the room, in the moment, and feeling what's happening is an advantage that only a human will ever have. A sense of humor, a sense of people, and a sense of the moment requires an actual heart, which the robots don't have. No offense, R2; here's another shot of espresso.

At our company, Peppercomm, we've been cultivating our comedy-based culture for more than fifteen years. During that time, we've transformed from a small, uptight, top-down organization to one in which the senior management team is always open to poking fun at themselves in the name of laughter. Our culture is based on the idea that a sense of humor is a secret weapon that bonds us in a way that no training program, magazine article, or prescription painkiller ever could.

Years ago, Steve pulled a prank on an employee we'll call Sabrina. Upon her return to NYC from a nice beach vacation, we congratulated her on being transferred to our San Francisco office, a move that she knew nothing about. There were balloons, greeting cards, a banner reading "Go West, Young Woman," and lots of emails thanking her for all of her excellent work here on the East Coast. She was simply gobsmacked at the outpouring of well-wishes and shocked that we would relocate her without even as much as a word of conversation about the move. Of course, we wouldn't do that, and we instantly let her off the hook Ashton Kutcher–style. She laughed out loud at how thoroughly we'd committed to the bit and immediately began plotting her revenge.

Steve, a few weeks later, was on a vacation of his own (what else is new?), and Sabrina went to work, whipping up a wicked brew her namesake teenage witch would envy. With the emotional roller coaster she'd ridden still fresh in her mind, she conspired with a few coworkers to stuff five thousand plastic balls that one might find in a local Chuck E. Cheese into Steve's office closet. When he returned to work, they waited for him to open that door, but as luck would have it, it was a warm day with no jacket required. The anticipation built and built, and it started to look like he'd never open that door and the payoff was not forthcoming. Never fear, though. Another employee, who was well known for always shivering at work in any temperature, asked the boss for a sweater to borrow. We all got our cameras ready as Steve proceeded to the closet to rescue this hypothermic colleague, and when he opened the door, it rained a deluge of plastic balls all over him that even Noah would have found intimidating. The entire office burst into hysterical laughter. Always a good sport,

Steve laughed along and even kept the balls all over the office for a week to let us know how funny it was to him. Revenge had been achieved and those balls were the talk of the office for a month.

From the beginning of time, ordinary citizens have taken it upon themselves to poke fun at the powerful. Politicians, leaders, and even kings have been the target of comedy for thousands of years.[1] Even the original leaders of the Ming Dynasty weren't immune to having fun poked at them any-time they messed up. From Yangtze to Banksy, the average person has always felt empowered to stand up and speak out through comedy.

Of course, with social and digital media, that once small pool of dissenters can now contain tens of millions! There are any number of examples in which a CEO posted a com-ment and then found himself the butt of countless sarcastic jokes that blew up the internet for multiple news cycles.[2] When this happens, the best defense is a good offense, and self-deprecating humor is an absolute godsend when a leader is targeted. The important thing is to own it and do so in a fun-loving way. Because of the shared language of comedy, leaders must learn to speak in that language.[3]

Clearly, Elon Musk only speaks in one language, and he alone knows what that language is.[4] His countless polarizing tweets have antagonized millions. Is it any wonder Tesla's stock fell 72 percent between November 2021 and January 2023 as Musk became an increasingly controversial public figure? Musk is an example of worst practices, and he abuses the basic tenets of comedy on social media to the detriment of himself, his companies, and his stakeholders.[5]

In this book, you will see how Peppercomm and other companies are using the various styles of comedy to achieve a higher ROI. It's not always easy to measure in terms of exact dollars (we can't say whether you've reached your monthly quota of chuckles and pay you a corresponding commission for doing so). But because we know that culture trumps everything else, the return is real, and laughter should be a fundamental part of your business plan. You may not have a CEO who would laugh at a closet full of plastic balls, but it is essential in today's workplace environment to have humor be present. Whether in person or on yet another Zoom call, *happy employees are the bottom line.*

Also in this book, we will explore CEOs who remain ambivalent when it comes to employees' concerns and desires. Just look at Starbucks[6] and Amazon[7] for the effect of leaders refusing to accept the realities and pitfalls of ignoring employee activism. These tone-deaf CEOs have chosen to not only ignore their employees' pleas for the protections that labor unions can provide; they're fighting back. But they're fighting a losing battle: in 2022, Starbucks boasted a turnover rate of 65 percent,[8] which pales in comparison to Amazon's stellar 150 percent.[9] We might need some more WD-40 for those revolving doors.

Happily, such companies are outliers when it comes to leadership. Leaders of today are increasingly in touch with their employees' desires and needs. A great example is Francesco Lagutaine, chief marketing, communications, and digital officer of M&T Bank (https://www3.mtb.com). Headquartered in Buffalo, the superregional bank has weathered many setbacks over the years. And believe us, in Buffalo, they know about weather! Francesco is a subject matter expert, both about snow and effective leadership. He says:

> Empathy is the name of the game. We all know 2022 was a tough year in Buffalo. Three years of house arrests, people sheltering in place, and all that kind of stuff. Despite having short commutes, turns out they still feel better at home. But there's a sense of isolation that comes from being home and, I believe, a loss of perspective. I'm in the office, but I have always needed that perspective. It's very important for people to look after one another, right? If I see someone who's miserable, who's always late, I can stop by and say, "Hey, what's up?" It's impossible to do that over Zoom.
>
> We've done a ton in the name of empathy. Every week I log in and I just tell people what I did in my week. Recognize some people for their work. It's a great way to keep things, keep people connected. It lets them know that I'm here with them and creates a sense of both empathy and vulnerability, right?
>
> I encourage people to look after one another. I tell people when I'm stressed out and I need time with my

family. I remind people what's important in life, like spending time with family, taking time out. People are more comfortable asking questions in the virtual space because you can be obviously more candid hidden behind the wall with your camera off.

We have a woman on my team who is a therapist by hobby. She's contributed her insights in so many ways that have improved our morale and connectivity. We organized a number of all-hands meetings, and she's even offered to provide one-on-one counseling to anyone here who reaches out to her. That sort of thing simply didn't happen before March 2020.

Going back to humor, for me, it works to take drama out of intense situations. I find humor to be a release, be it gallows humor, a self-deprecating joke I might make about my English, or letting people know we're all in the same space, we're in it together. Don't let stress consume your life; try to sort of hover above it. I think using humor at work helps a lot with that.

Francesco knows what we've always known, that happy employees are the key to any company's success. M&T, a company that has posted profits every year since 1976, is led by a CEO whose favorability rating is an almost unheard of 80 percent.[10] And employees rate the company 4.0 out of 5.[11] Clearly, they've struck the right balance, and that's what this book is all about, finding the right balance for your organization. It's not profits over people, nor is it people over profits. The ROI of LOL is people and profits!

2

PEPPERCOMM'S HISTORY
WITH COMEDY TRAINING

OUR RELATIONSHIP WITH comedy began as a result of Steve's ongoing midlife crisis, which started when he was a junior in high school. During this forty-year refusal to grow up, Steve has thus far ticked off many of the stereotypical male menopause-avoidance boxes, including (but most certainly not limited to):

- Tooling around in a little red sports car
- Finding anyone with natural or bleached blond hair to hop into the passenger seat of said little red sports car
- Climbing three of the world's Seven Summits as well as rock and ice climbing everywhere from the Andes to the Alps

Having failed to satiate his appetite for validation, sometime around the turn of the century (that would be the twenty-first century), Steve stumbled into a weeklong stand-up comedy workshop in a dingy office building near

Penn Station on Manhattan's not-so-glamorous West Side. The goal? To write and perform five minutes of material at a New York City nightclub at the end of the week.

Thus the training began for a motley and ragtag group of high school students, retired cops, corporate lawyers, and one very nervous owner of a public relations firm who was wondering what the hell he'd gotten himself into.

✶ ✶ ✶ ✶ ✶ ROI TIP *from* STEVE ✶ ✶ ✶ ✶ ✶ ✶

MY FIRST FORAY into becoming a comedy writer had me reconsidering all my life decisions up to that point. What was I thinking signing up for this torture? My assignment was to jot down three or four things that ticked me off to get the juices flowing. If memory serves, my list included:

- My annual two-week summer vacation in a godforsaken, bug-ridden, and bat-infested camp in the wilds of Maine owned by my wife and her siblings (each of whom spent the entire fortnight reliving the memories of their misspent youth)

- The trials and tribulations of rooting for the perennially abysmal New York Jets and Mets

- The occasional a**hole client

Note: The latter two remain irritations, but I've been blissfully Maine free since 2003.

The anticipation I felt on the day of my stand-up debut was beyond agonizing. It was arguably the most nerve-racking day of my life. The time came, and I took the stage. When I tell you the fear almost killed me, I'm not exaggerating.

But I survived.

I stumbled through my material, received a decidedly muted reaction from the audience, and dashed outside, beyond relieved that I'd ticked off yet another bucket list item. Or had I?

The emcee of the show approached me, told me he'd enjoyed my set, and described my performance as "not half bad." He mentioned that he hosted his own show at a different club and asked if I'd like to perform there with him the very next Friday night. Would I ever! Almost immediately, inane *A Star Is Born* thoughts ricocheted through my brain: *A professional comedian thinks I'm good and wants me to perform on his show. Next stop: Conan, Kimmel, and my very own HBO special.* The emcee, as you may have guessed by now, was Clayton, my coauthor. And although I still haven't received a single call from any late-night talent booker, the two of us have been performing together ever since.

A funny thing happened as a result of this unlikely union of a CEO and a comedy club veteran. As we worked on Steve's material, reviewing videos of his performances and talking about how to improve his timing, delivery, and laughs per minute, Steve noticed that doing comedy recurrently was having a profound, positive effect on his business communications skills. We began to think just maybe we were on to something.

When it comes to truly connecting with an audience and creating a positive-feedback loop, there are ten things every comedian knows that every business executive should know:

1. How to build compelling, confident presentation skills
2. How to listen and observe actively and effectively
3. How to be truthful and compelling in storytelling
4. How to get a conversation back on course
5. How to get someone who's multitasking or otherwise distracted to pay attention
6. How to display authenticity, empathy, vulnerability, and transparency
7. How to handle objections or hostility from a group or an individual
8. How to close a sale/move your audience toward your desired outcome
9. How to stimulate innovative and creative thinking
10. How to differentiate yourself as a leader or your company as a brand

How many of these, dear reader, are applicable to your current challenges?

We realized together that great comedians are, at their core, expert communicators. It became clear that everyone at Steve's public relations firm, Peppercomm, would benefit from the very same comedy training he had received. Soon after, Clayton was named Peppercomm's first chief comedy officer. To this day, he trains all Peppercomm employees in the fundamental techniques of stand-up comedy, improvisational comedy, and sketch comedy. He also participates regularly in our brainstorming sessions, directs our ridiculous comedy videos, and generally helps us with anything we're doing that shows our humorous side.

As a result of this unexpected partnership, comedy became baked into our firm's DNA, and it quickly became clear there was a ravenous appetite for humor in the larger business world. We began garnering attention from the media. MSNBC ran a ten-minute segment[1] on how we'd leveraged comedy to create our unique workplace culture. *Fast Company* wrote a feature about us,[2] as did the *New York Post*.[3] *Crain's New York Business* even named Peppercomm the best workplace of the year, topping 960 other entries including Google, Microsoft, and New York Life.[4] The agency also made the list in 2021 and 2022.

Before long, our clients began asking us to develop comedy integration and training programs for their leadership teams, sales forces, human resources, and communications departments.

Some of our employees join Steve and Clayton performing in comedy clubs all over New York. One is Senior Vice President Rob Duda, who remembers the day he made his own real comedy debut: "Just a few weeks after my first comedy training session, you guys talked me into trying it for real. It was so different from when we had the class; this time I didn't know a person in the crowd. But I took the leap and soon people I didn't even know were laughing at my jokes. It was an amazing feeling. Now when I get up to present in front of a room of business colleagues, I feel confident and at ease."

WHAT SETS US APART

Companies of all types come to us for one compelling reason: we provide the integrated viewpoints and skills of both a corporate senior executive and a full-time professional entertainer. As a result, we are able to immediately connect with corporate leaders, teams, and individual contributors on how to master comedy techniques to overcome real-world business challenges. So our focus is practical and not like the countless improv troupes that would be more than happy to take your money to send you an instructor to loosen up your employees for a day.

Over the years, we have worked with many different types of professionals and situations:

- Doctors and nurses who had devoted their careers to treating stage 4 cancer patients but needed help improving listening skills, empathy, and bedside manner.

- A defense contractor whose rocket engineers were routinely described as "merchants of death" at their neighborhood barbecues and cocktail parties. We taught them how to use humor to redirect the conversation and deflect the attack like a Patriot missile.

- A behemoth oral care conglomerate whose separate dental floss and toothpaste divisions didn't like or communicate with each other but shared a mutual disgust for the mouthwash team. We helped them break down the plaque in their corporate silos and get to the root (canal) of the problem.

Our various comedy training programs provided a fun outlet and a nice revenue stream for Peppercomm until March 2020. Then, as the entire world was confronted with the uncertainty of a global pandemic, Peppercomm's comedy service offerings morphed from a nice-to-have to a need-to-have. Companies began calling us to help their employees better cope with heretofore unseen levels of stress, fear, depression, loneliness, anxiety, and working in a world of 24/7 bad news.

Now that so many organizations have evolved into the remote/hybrid working model (and with many signs indicating this will be a permanent shift), we're using comedy training to connect leaders, teams, and individuals who were hired before the pandemic with those who have only ever interacted over Zoom meetings. We're helping to bridge divides between various generations, blue-collar plant workers and their PhD peers, employees with widely differing political opinions, and all other groups of opposites that are so often called upon to come together to collaborate.

But those are just the employee-engagement outcomes we are producing for clients. We're also using comedy techniques to craft compelling, award-winning PR and marketing campaigns and leveraging our comedy skills to train brands and their internal experts to brainstorm like comedians in a writers' room, to create their own breakthrough campaigns. That's a major benefit for any organization looking to deepen existing ties with customers or initiate new ones with top prospects.

In the chapters that follow, we'll take a deeper dive into exactly how we do what we do, how the tenets of comedy can be tailored to meet the specific needs of your organization, how to measure the cost benefit of comedy training, and how it can enhance corporate storytelling in unexpected ways that will enable you to better connect with every stakeholder audience.

Oh, and for those of you who may just be starting your own business or work in a smallish organization that can't afford Clayton's outrageously high fees (not to mention unreasonable demands for celebrity stylists and blue M&M's in his greenroom), we'll also show you how to create your own comedy-driven workplace culture.

By the way, have you heard the one about the guy whose midlife crisis began in high school?

3

THE POWER OF LAUGHTER

WE'VE ALL HEARD that laughter is good medicine. We know that laughter relieves stress, increases oxygen flow, and boosts overall health. In the American Physiological Society's excellent journal *Advances in Physiology Education*, we learn that laughter "is part of a universal language of basic emotions that all humans recognize."[1] We know about the countless other studies that have been done to support the idea of getting your high-dosage laughter prescription refilled as often as possible. Most of all, we know that laughing feels good. But have you ever considered why?

There are many neuroscientific explanations for why going "ha ha ha" makes us feel so great, and they all revolve around the healing power of peptides like oxytocin and neurotransmitters like serotonin.[2] These "feel good" chemicals trigger the release of endorphins, which are hormones in the brain that activate opiate receptors throughout your body and mind. Endorphins ease pain in the body, reduce stress, and create a sense of euphoria. They are seven times more powerful than morphine, and they're much easier to get.

The six ways to achieve the natural high of an endorphin rush are:

1. Aerobic exercise
2. Consuming certain foods like dark chocolate
3. Adrenaline-based activities like skydiving
4. Narcotics, including heroin and cocaine (which we don't recommend)
5. Laughing out loud
6. Our favorite, falling in love[3]

It's important to note that in the moment of endorphin release, the brain does not differentiate among the various stimuli. This means that, in a very real way, when someone makes you laugh, you fall in love with that person for a moment. If you really want someone to fall in love with you, tell her a joke while feeding her chocolate while she's bungee jumping off a StairMaster!

Comedians see this "love potion" effect of laughter every night in comedy clubs around the world. It's very common for audience members to line up to request hugs from a hilarious performer or possibly even tell their life stories, despite not having even officially met. Of course, the two-drink minimum helps with this, but something else is at play: the bonding effect of sharing a laugh.

* * * * * * **LOL TIP** *from* **CLAYTON** * * * * * *

ONE NIGHT MANY years ago, I had just gotten off the stage at New York Comedy Club. A woman of a certain age approached me, hand outstretched. "I really needed that. I lost my husband five days ago." I replied, "Want me to help you find him?" She laughed and told me that coming to the show that night was the first step she'd taken toward healing after her husband lost his three-year battle with cancer.

We chatted for a few minutes, and during that conversation I learned her name was Winnie and her late husband's name was Don. We talked about how long they'd lived in the neighborhood, what local restaurants they liked, how they each felt about the mayor, and so on. It was a long and tender, bittersweet conversation. I realized during our chat that I had somehow helped her begin to forget the saddest day of her life and start to heal and move on. It was the first time I truly understood why people say laughter is the best medicine. It felt so good to know I was helping this woman overcome her burden.

She shared, "I'm all cried out and figured it was time to try laughing. I'm so glad I came to this place tonight. You cheered me up and I can't thank you enough for the show." I said, "You gonna buy my CD or what?" She laughed again, pretended she was about to smack me, and instead reached for her purse. I stopped her and gave her the CD for free because what she gave me that night was worth a lot more. And that's not saying much, believe me.

My interaction with Winnie made me realize that the work we comics do is important. Before that chat with my newly widowed friend, I saw this job as something I enjoyed but that was ultimately selfish. "Hey, everybody, look at me, give me attention, listen to me talk into this

> microphone, me me me!" That night, Winnie taught me how wrong I was to view performing in comedy clubs as a zero-sum endeavor.
>
> I still think of her often and wish I'd charged her for that CD.

Think about your best friend or someone else you really love to have around you. We're willing to bet that you and that person share a similar sense of humor. Perhaps you both enjoy the same Kevin Hart movie or agree on which Amy Schumer punch line is the funniest. Maybe you even share inside jokes about someone in your group chat's new boyfriend. You have probably laughed together more than once about a pet peeve you have in common. Laughter is a powerful bonding agent indeed.[4]

Rupen Desai, cofounder of The Shed 28 and former chief marketing officer (CMO) at Dole Sunshine Company, takes this idea even further, and unapologetically so: "I have a rule to only work with people I like. Yeah, and I know this is terribly wrong because business forces you to work with people whose personalities clash with your own. We've gotta be able to work with everybody, right? Wrong! I've come to measure people on: Do they give me oxygen, or do they take away oxygen from me?" Which one are you at the office, the giver or the taker? You don't want your coworkers waiting to exhale every time you suck the "O" out of every meeting, physical, virtual, or otherwise.

Even when it comes to romantic relationships, or what psychologists call pair bonding, a sense of humor plays an enormous role. There is a reason why more than 90 percent of all dating app users list "sense of humor" as a highly desired trait.[5] There's even a dating app called Smile, which matches couples based purely on what they both find funny.[6] It turns out the good old funny stuff is absolutely essential in pair bonding. A University of Kansas study found that a man's overall batting average in terms of how often a woman he just met laughs at his jokes is a surprisingly direct indicator of their overall attraction and compatibility.[7] The study's lead researcher, Associate Professor of Communication Studies Jeffrey Hall, determined that "the idea that humor is a signal of intelligence doesn't give humor its due credit." Indeed, it goes much further than just a way to show your brainpower; this is about finding your potential soulmate. Hall explains, "If you meet someone who you can laugh with, it might mean your future relationship is going to be fun and filled with good cheer." Even the legendary Audrey Hepburn once said, "I love people who make me laugh. I honestly think it's the thing I like most. It cures a multitude of ills. It's probably the most important thing in a person."

So why does laughing together create such adhesion? It works because no one wants to feel alone, and laughing together is a clear way of finding common ground, expressing agreement, and showing sympathy. And it's always 100 percent honest because true laughter is involuntary. We all want to feel connected to one another. How many times have we heard comedians utter the phrase, "Who's with me?" This comes from the innate human desire to be understood, acknowledged, and validated.[8]

Visionary business leaders are also coming around to the importance of laughing at work. Our friend and longtime client Peter Weedfald, who is also the author of *Green Reign*

Leadership and senior vice president of sales and marketing at SHARP Home Electronics Marketing Company of America, states, "Laughter and smiles are not just icebreakers in business. We all know from personal experience that hearty laughter causes heartfelt smiles and fuels ardent happiness in our busy lives. In business, and for leaders in particular, jaunty spirited humor mollifies and promotes unity across every part of an organization. Return on investment in sales, marketing, and business cannot be simply measured through financial results, through the cold steel of the P&L. Absent humor, business struggles to enjoy the greater spirit of opportunity in the language of kinetic goodwill."

But in the workplace, just as in society as a whole, we are increasingly shying away from levity.[9] The use of one's sense of humor in a serious business discourse or a similar setting is seen as somehow unprofessional or inappropriate. Comedy itself is always changing (much of what was funny ten years ago wouldn't get a chuckle today), but so is its broader role in society. Despite laughter's many well-documented benefits, scientists estimate that we're laughing 70 percent less today than we did in the depths of the Great Depression in the 1930s.[10] The average toddler laughs four hundred times per day. The average forty-year-old needs two months to reach the same total![11]

So, what's going on in this chuckle-deficient world anyway? The factors contributing to our broken funny bone are too numerous to compile, but some are:

- Disconnectedness from other people due to virtual work
- Widespread addiction to social media
- Sensitivity and political correctness

- Anxiety over job security due to massive layoffs across many sectors
- Compound responsibilities and unrealistic expectations
- The mistaken idea that if you're having too much fun you must not be working hard enough

Put it all together and it starts to feel like the only one enjoying life on Earth is your nephew who's still in day care.

Now we're not asserting here that we should all be laughing hysterically all day like a room filled with toddlers. We are just saying that the trend is heading in the wrong direction, and we're doing our part to change that. By developing and using your unique, personal sense of humor in appropriate ways at appropriate times, you can stand out in business and in life like a toddler who can play Beethoven's *Eroica* Symphony on the toy piano.

* * * * * * ROI TIP *from* STEVE * * * * * *

I'VE USED SELF-DEPRECATING humor to break through and connect with very powerful and very serious chief communications officers (CCOs) and CMOs who are members of my profession's two top trade organizations.

I'm fortunate to serve on the board of both groups and unfortunate to have to attend some painfully boring board meetings. As I observe the back-and-forth banter, I use my listening skills to inject an unexpectedly funny, but relevant, point to the conversation. In many instances, my comments not only stop these serious taskmasters in their tracks but completely change the energy and enthusiasm in the meeting. Often one of my comments will lead to a series of other unexpectedly funny observations from the CCOs and CMOs. And, critically, I slowly develop trust and confidence with my peers (who are often prospective clients).

At an industry trade association board meeting, I was one of two executive committee members who were asked to step up to the front of the conference room and accept specially engraved plaques saluting our service. The other was Dave, a longtime, well-respected colleague of mine. As soon as the applause died, I said, "This is an especially awkward moment, since Dave and I absolutely despise each other." The silence was deafening for a beat, and then everyone roared with laughter. Many of them started adding onto the running gag of how we all despised one another, in a clearly good-natured way.

Bottom line: I'm now expected to inject humor in most board meetings I attend, and my firm has won significant business as a direct result of my using humor to create the camaraderie and trust necessary for a *Fortune* 500 CCO to retain my firm. It's important to note that without my self-deprecating funny bone, Peppercomm would almost never be considered as an agency partner by many of these organizations (who typically hire publicly traded, global agencies to do their bidding).

To be seen as a forward-thinking, charismatic leader in any organization requires you to learn to humanize yourself and become more relatable by applying the comedy skills explored in this book. Rather than an adversarial relationship between managers and the employee base, you create a feeling of fraternity.[12]

As business leaders, we use comedy skills to communicate to our teams that we're all in this together, as evidenced by the fact that we all agree that the security officer in the office building talks too loudly. We've laughed together about how the migration to the new server didn't go so smoothly. And our CCO had us all in stitches about what her four-year-old triplets did over the weekend. As the laughter flows, so does the work.

Stacey Jones of Accenture put it better than we ever could: "I've found that humor is key to diffusing stress. Sometimes meetings go on for too long or nothing fabulous arises from brainstorming. In times like those, it's critical to help people relax or to break the tension in the room—and humor can do it. Humor also helps get us out of a 'loop' that drags down creativity so we can open up thinking. But it's important to remember that humor doesn't have to come from leaders. I love it when someone on my team just cracks us up with a witticism or joke or funny 'take' on the situation. It brings us together and boosts morale."

Creating a collaborative workplace culture in which laughter is not only allowed but expected is an important step in building what we call TOAST:

Trust
Openness

Authenticity
Storytelling
Teamwork

TOAST (with or without butter) is essential to any healthy collaborative environment.

A study published in the American Psychological Association's *Journal of Applied Psychology* found that humor triggers "positive socioemotional communication, procedural structure, and new solutions."[13] The use of levity improved team performance in both the short and the long term. This was particularly true in what the researchers identified as "low job insecurity climate conditions," or what we identify as offices where employees aren't overly concerned with getting the ax. This makes perfect sense to us, and we'll delve into this area more fully in the next chapter.

What all this means for your business is that by harnessing the prodigious power of your own unique individual sense of humor, and empowering your employees to do the same, you can increase morale, collaboration, communication, and productivity. You can find new and unexpected ways to connect with your external stakeholders. And you can have fun doing it.

A little love potion goes a long way.

FIVE CHARACTERISTICS OF
A HEALTHY WORKPLACE CULTURE

THE WHOLE IDEA of work is evolving before our very eyes. Gone are the days of punching a time card and having the boss man scream at you for eight hours. Today's forward-looking employers know they have to compete to keep the best and brightest, and 76 percent of candidates rank a healthy workplace culture as a higher priority than any other determinant, even including salary and benefits![1]

So, what does a healthy culture look like? As mentioned previously, we believe there are five essential elements that must be in place: Trust, Openness, Authenticity, Storytelling, and Teamwork.

TRUST

It probably doesn't come as news to anyone reading this that trust is important in any workplace. For decades, companies have tried to manufacture trust through silly games like falling backward and hoping Marc from the mailroom knows how to catch. Engaging in a "trust fall" or carrying an egg across the room on a spoon doesn't actually bring people closer together. These exercises are contrived and predictable enough to be considered boring by most savvy employees.

Trust at work is built over time, through awareness of, and respect for, employees' expectations, boundaries, and opinions. When your coworkers feel free to fail in front of you, when they see time and time again that you have faith in their abilities, and when you show them repeatedly that you will have their backs, trust is present. Only in this environment can true creativity occur because, as every comedic performer knows, mistakes are the building blocks of innovation. Success can occur only through the process of trial and error, so mistakes and failures must be embraced. After all, lessons are learned through these mistakes and failures.

We once had a very intelligent and capable account supervisor named Lola (not her real moniker, obviously; this isn't 1906), who wasn't content with just being an account supervisor. Lola was the day-to-day account manager on a major manufacturing account for us that had manufactured itself a major PR crisis. We're not talking bad; we're talking really bad, as in polluting the major waterways of the greater New England area by dumping carcinogens into them.

The news media were all over the story. Even Erin Brockovich crashed these events, as did many other well-known environmentalists, angry townspeople whose farm animals were getting sick, and other concerned citizens. We had to act quickly. Our very best minds met every morning, reviewed what had happened the day before, and compiled a list of suggested statements for the client to use in press conferences.

For example, our senior executives huddled and developed such authentic messages as: "We are committed to cleaning up the mess we have caused, and we're also going to provide funds to help the sick farm animals and support the local farmers affected by the pollution." Another gem: "Our CEO himself is going to each town to meet with citizens and local politicians face-to-face to personally apologize." Of course he was mugged a few times in places like Merrimac, New Hampshire, and Albany, New York, but the fact that he showed up at all demonstrated the company's regret around the terrible incident.

Lola not only listened to our senior executives' ideas but, like a snake in a polluted swamp, *presented them as her own to the client*. Needless to say, the client absolutely loved "Lola's" recommendations, and we began receiving dozens of emails from the client praising Lola and thanking us for her creative and timely solutions and thinking. When confronted, Lola denied that she had stolen our ideas and passed them off as her own, but at that point the waters were already poisoned. In fact, she'd done such a good job of conning the client that they hired her away from us, and she allegedly still counsels them today.

Lesson learned. Importantly, we don't actually want someone working at our firm who can't be trusted, and Lola is missed about as much as a five-foot-deep pothole on Manhattan's FDR Drive.

The strongest bonds of trust can be built through laughter. By taking the risk of making a joke at work, you subtly communicate that you: (a) want someone to feel good; and (b) trust that she will "get" the tone of your quip and appreciate it. Anytime we build relationships in life, an element of trust must be present in order for the relationship to go anywhere, and laughter is a great way to start building those bonds.[2]

At Peppercomm, our chief talent officer, Tara Lilien, emphasizes the importance of trust in all that we do, highlighting that it "allows us to operate in an environment where we can be direct with each other. We are able to build that trust through our day-to-day interactions because we know each other so well. Every company says, 'we're a family,' but we really do see ourselves this way."

Often, a little levity is especially useful before the difficult conversations all leaders have to have with their direct reports from time to time. That human touch makes the exchange more productive and ensures the message sent is the message received. Rather than being dejected, the employee leaves feeling motivated and focused on success in the areas addressed. The relationship is already solid because trust has been built long before the difficult conversation even starts. This is very important because without that trust, the employee might automatically take a defensive position, perhaps wanting to justify or explain any mistakes that had been made for fear of being fired over them. When that happens, listening and learning are severely hindered.

Around here, we build trust through real human connection. By laughing together, working together, disagreeing together, having fun together, and occasionally crying together, we create genuine trust at work.

So leave the blindfolds, potato sack races, and hard-boiled eggs to the amateurs.

OPENNESS

The word is out that openness is important, but it means more than just spreading out the furniture in your workspace or installing a glass door to your CEO's office. True openness comes from a willingness to listen to feedback, suggestions, ideas, and even criticism from your entire staff. Your workplace culture is open if everyone doesn't get silent the moment a C-suite executive enters the break room.

In her wonderful book *The Fearless Organization*, Harvard professor Amy Edmondson discusses the need for what she calls "psychological safety" in the workplace. Edmondson feels that in order for true dynamic innovation to take place, there must first be a culture in which "people feel accepted and comfortable sharing concerns and mistakes without fear of embarrassment or retribution." Without that psychological safety, openness is impossible because employees will resort to self-protective tactics designed to limit risks and accountability.

"Members of innovative teams may think of themselves like the inspiring teacher who pushed them to be their best," she writes. "They feel safe to speak up when they see things differently, and they willingly push one another to be the best as they pursue common goals. They openly debate ideas and take decisive action, but they do so in ways that help team members maintain respect for one another. . . . They are able to set aside their egos and change their minds when presented with evidence that favors another viewpoint."[3]

Lilien agrees wholeheartedly with Edmondson's take, adding: "If an intern, a middle manager, and a partner walk into Steve's office [or how about a priest, rabbi, and minister?] at the same time, each will receive an equal opportunity to share, brainstorm, and opine, and the best idea wins regardless of the source from which it came." At Peppercomm, we all listen to one another regardless of status or position within the company. We respect and give space to all opinions, especially those with which we happen to disagree.

Every company has a hierarchy, or organizational chart, defining whose role is what and who answers to whom. We're not suggesting this isn't important, but we've learned that a wide range of styles can exist within a company's structure:

- Does your company make decisions from the top down?
- Does your CEO send out a weekly email implying severe consequences for anyone who doesn't follow the rule of the week?
- Is the CEO open to suggestions on how to improve internal communication or ways to increase workflow?
- Does your company truly have an open-door policy, or is someone at or near the top on a power trip?
- Do your employees feel free to express themselves or is everyone just trying not to get fired?

If your culture is truly open, communication flows up, down, and sideways—and even those in the C-suite are happy to listen to new ideas and constructive criticism.

A real test of openness is organizational change. Today, any business that expects to grow is likely to require at least some transformation, and that is seldom easy on the people involved. Jobs change. Jobs get eliminated. People's titles change. They report to new people. Where many companies go wrong in the midst of all these changes is they become secretive. In their desperate attempts to protect workers from any sense of disruption that may arise from the process, they plan changes in covert meetings behind closed doors over a period of months. And then, one day, out of the blue, they spring the "new normal" on their direct reports all at once. Surprise!

We've seen countless companies unintentionally fall victim to this "black box" mentality. Executives are so committed to secrecy, they create plans for change in a vacuum rather than engaging the people who are in a position to know what changes would actually be best for the company. The people who are supposed to change, and the people responsible for making the change happen, are never consulted about the change before it's already in motion.

Is anybody shocked that, by most estimates, 70 percent of all change initiatives fail?[4] We didn't think so. And what's the top reason change initiatives fail? A recent study by *Harvard Business Review* and Strativity found it to be due to poor communication.[5] Again, not a shocker.

What you *might* be shocked to learn, though, is how we applied an incredibly innovative approach to change management for one of our clients that was really struggling to effect a new initiative.

The Fast-Track Program: A Case Study

A major business consulting firm approached us one day about a program they had introduced with much fanfare and great expectations. This "fast-track" program was expected to have a significant effect on retention of high performers and client growth.

The idea was to give senior managers the opportunity to advance their skills in client relationship management through a mentorship program. Top executives within the company would mentor these senior managers and provide opportunities to engage with clients and, eventually, take on books of business assignments that were, up until that point, the sole responsibility of the mentors.

The program, it was hoped, would help top performers build important qualifications, strengthen client bonds, and position themselves for promotion within the company. It would simultaneously help the executives by freeing up their calendars a bit in a time when they were all spread far too thin. Sounds like a win-win, right?

Just one problem: the C-suite executives who built this program forgot to ask anyone for input on how to make it a success.

Oops.

The targeted, fast-tracked managers didn't understand the program or their role in it. Senior leaders were skeptical that they would benefit from using some of their already very limited time to mentor anyone. They were also understandably reluctant to hand over parts of their portfolios of business to their junior counterparts.

Though some fast-tracked individuals embraced the program from the outset, most felt blindsided by it. Many we consulted felt that the potential for growth was there, but with limited information on program elements and benefits, it was going to be a struggle. The program launch was a disaster.

Where had our client gone wrong?

The program's creators could have conducted a survey or hosted focus groups in hopes of gathering input from invested parties on how to implement this big mentorship idea. They could have sat down with potential fast-track candidates to gauge interest and expectations. They could have spoken with the business leaders ahead of time and allowed them to share their concerns over time commitment, confidentiality, and desired outcomes. They could have tested the big idea with a smaller group in a different market, gotten feedback, and then made improvements before a company-wide rollout. They didn't do any of these things, and the entire program was in jeopardy as a result.

Enter Peppercomm with a mandate to cocreate a new program through a process we call Mixology (yes, it's like making cool drinks). Our Mixology process consists of three sessions, each with a different goal in mind.

When participants entered the first virtual session, they were greeted with live music and introduced to professional improv actors. These performers brought to life the experiences participants were having, but in a fun, abstract way.

For example, the freedom to tailor mentor/mentee plans without much guidance was brought to life onstage as freedom to travel where you like but with no map to help you get there. Participants laughed at the improv performances. Everyone was amazed at the talented musicians and how spot-on applicable the beautiful music they improvised was to the problems being addressed. The scenes brought the issues around this initiative to life. Relaxed and engaged, participants opened up to us and offered valuable insights on what a mentorship program in their company could be, if done right.

A second session focused on creating solutions based on what had surfaced in the first session. We led an epic, improvisational brainstorm in which no idea could be counted as too ridiculous, expensive, or off the wall. Such negativity was strictly against the rules. Working with senior leadership, potential fast-track candidates, and our own comedic performers, we came up with an outline for what success would look like.

The final piece was a detailed road map for a new program based on the one that was, at that point, in shambles. We spent a day working with employees at all levels of the proposed fast-track program and, along with its original architects, developed a plan of implementation that took everyone's thoughts, feedback, and concerns into consideration. Everyone expressed optimism that we might be able to save the dead-on-arrival initiative, after all, but we'd have to sell it to the rest of the company.

Within a day or two, word of our incredibly unorthodox Mixology workshops had already spread throughout the company. Although fewer than a hundred employees had taken part in the sessions, we quickly learned that word of mouth had already reenergized all two thousand program participants. By the time our new road map was delivered, employees across all levels had eagerly bought in.

Today, that program thrives and has even won several workplace culture awards. We don't think we could have resurrected it without comedy.

AUTHENTICITY

Once upon a time in corporate America, the standard protocol for handling uncharted waters was "fake it till you make it." Executives didn't want to be seen as weak or anything less than omniscient, so they took great measures to avoid the appearance of being in any way flawed. As the culture of America itself moved away from the glamorous fantasy world of *Dynasty* and into the more realistic themes of *Duck Dynasty*, so did the American workplace.

Today's comedy club audiences, like their streaming-service audience counterparts, expect a level of reality more transparent and honest than at any time in the history of entertainment. Gone are the days of the Hollywood starlet in a mink stole calling everyone "darling" and puffing an impossibly slender cigarette. Today, we watch as DJ Pauly D dates multiple women in Las Vegas, Amy Schumer cooks dinner with her husband, and everyone tries to keep up with the Kardashians. The curtain has been pulled back, and it's not closing anytime soon.

As the idea of privacy continues its steady march toward obsolescence, corporate leaders must embrace the office version of authenticity.[6] Even as we peer into each other's homes during Zoom meetings, facades that would have been considered polite and even necessary as recently as a decade ago must now be stripped away. Reality culture is permeating comedy, music, social media, theater, and fine art. It must also find its way into the modern corporate space or else employees will feel detached from the company. Everyone says his organization is like a family, but building a family at work requires a level of honesty the CEOs of yore would have considered dangerous.

By the way, as it pertains to virtual meetings, we at Peppercomm have been pushing a "video-on" initiative for three years. For a company that is pretty liberal about so many corporate policies, we're downright adamant about showing our pretty faces to each other on Microsoft Teams. "It goes to staying connected and being our real selves with and for one another," asserts Lilien. A recent survey showed that 48 percent of American workers keep their cameras off when they're collaborating over Zoom.[7] We think 52 percent have it right.

* * * * * * ROI TIP *from* STEVE * * * * * *

AS THE PANDEMIC reached and surpassed the three-year mark, a sizable portion of our employee base remained completely or almost completely remote. So we still spend quite a lot of time on Teams. One of the ways we strengthen and build bonds in this virtual environment is by holding weekly staff meetings that are very brief. We call them the 12@12: twelve minutes a day at twelve noon twice a week. During the first 12@12, we spend time updating everyone on the business. But, on the second 12@12, we ask each of our people to spend twelve minutes giving "shout-outs" to each other. It's amazing to see one account team after another give virtual kudos to someone who has gone above and beyond to score a major article in *USA Today*, surprise and delight a client with a great idea, or simply be there to provide support for an ill colleague. 'Tis a beautiful thing to see unfold.

During the depths of the pandemic, our employees talked about how they were coping with the isolation. They answered questions like who they'd really like to quarantine with, their craziest Teams or Zoom experience, new hobbies, favorite binge watch, embarrassing moments, favorite foods, and so on. We encouraged them to add visuals and even ask trivia questions about themselves. Everyone got into the spirit, and we tried our best to enjoy our virtual office as much as the real one.

Even as pandemic lockdowns eased and our people began returning to the office once or twice a week, our staff literally begged us to continue the 12@12. Why? Because they love sharing stories about their lives that don't revolve around filling out timesheets and who can write the craftiest client email.

A funny thing happened on the way to the pandemic, though. Due in large part to these 12@12 meetings, I actually became far more connected to my employees than ever before, and I found myself making stronger connections with colleagues I had known for many years. It may seem odd that we became closer as a family without being physically together in our traditional shared space, but it's true.

We built new running inside jokes. For example, one of our Raleigh, NC-based employees, Paul, knows I'm a huge Mets fan. He made a point of antagonizing me by showing his loyalty to the rival Bronx Bombers in the form of a Yankees cap. He doesn't just wear it; he takes it off in the middle of our meetings and holds it right up to the camera, taunting me mercilessly every time the Mets lose. A West Coast employee named Hannah always seems to have a question right before sign-off. Now, I end every meeting with, "Any questions, Hannah?" even when she's not on the call.

Being authentic with each other is very important to our culture, virtual and otherwise. And the running jokes we've built on that authenticity keep us laughing through the madness.

THE ROI OF LOL

Axel Hefer, then CEO of one of Peppercomm's most important clients, trivago, brought his full, authentic self to a live interview on CNN.[8] We had secured a two-minute interview for Axel to discuss travel during the pandemic. To his credit, Axel realized that if trivago continued its marketing efforts while all their competitors shut theirs down because no one was traveling, trivago would remain front of mind throughout the lockdown.

We were thrilled to have landed this TV spot for him. About a minute into the interview, though, the CEO's four-year-old son decided to interrupt the proceedings and photobomb his dad, whose attention he was desperately and understandably craving. While many executives in his shoes on live television would have freaked out, Axel didn't miss a beat. He reached down, picked up his child, plopped him on his lap, and continued the interview as though his son weren't even there! The reporter adored this real-life moment, and the interview went viral. Trivago gained market share almost immediately after the travel restrictions were lifted.

How authentic are you willing to be, warts and all?

In one of our recent stand-up training sessions, a Peppercomm senior vice president felt so comfortable with her peers that she shared a very embarrassing story about a Caribbean vacation with her boyfriend where everything that could go wrong did. Her colleagues in the audience absolutely loved it, and she expressed that she felt free to share her whole self. In most companies, employees are expected to keep their love lives and their work lives completely separate, but here we don't have those barriers (within reason).

As we see it, letting the truth live and breathe is the key. Reed Hastings, chairman of Netflix, insists on authenticity in his company's culture.[9] Regarding failure, Hastings writes in his eye-opening tell-all, *No Rules Rules*, "When you sunshine your failed bets, everyone wins. You win because people learn they can trust you to tell the truth and to take responsibility for your actions. The team wins because it learns from the lessons that came out of the project. And the company wins because everyone sees clearly that failed bets are an inherent part of an innovative success wheel."

Learning to be more authentic in all conversations is critical to the success of any leader. As you will soon learn, great comedians are masters of honesty. Learning to use your sense of humor in the right way at the right time for the right audience is a fundamental skill to success in the future of work. We've seen dozens of business executives whose introverted personalities had stalled their career paths move up the proverbial corporate ladder after using these key skills to enhance their own personal charisma. Let's be honest: we all prefer to work with people whose company we enjoy, and a sense of humor is a key tool in developing that likability.

As Angela Sullivan, head of communications for the Americas at global cloud-software developer Xero (www .xero.com), puts it, "I generally tend to keep things light, personally and professionally. I believe that making others feel comfortable, and encouraging them to smile and to have fun, is way more motivating than being super serious all of the time. I like to laugh, and I like to make others laugh too!"

Humor can help lighten up a tense situation, but it requires reading the room to make the call on whether humor could be appropriate or not. "For me, it's a gut feeling," Sullivan continues. "It's not always right, as I've tripped over myself in the past with humor that went nowhere, but I've also been successful cracking a joke or two to break the ice in new situations. Don't take yourself too seriously. There's so much benefit to encouraging laughter day to day."

Authenticity at work starts at the top. You've got to ignore your inner Jack Nicholson saying your employees can't handle the truth. You have to trust them to do just that, or else they won't trust you at all, and then your corporate culture isn't toasting anything! The facts come out soon enough anyway, so just be honest from the start. As the Buddha once said, "Three things cannot long be hidden: the sun, the moon, and the truth."

STORYTELLING

Virtually every company that engages Peppercomm expresses a strong desire to improve their corporate storytelling. But most are very conservative and cautious in terms of not saying, speaking, or sharing any word, phrase, or idea that might possibly offend or upset any one of a myriad of stakeholder audiences. We believe that you've got to take a stand on what your messaging is. Being overly cautious in this area leads to mundane, bland content that gets little or no attention. If you want to stand out, you have to stand up.

One key role of storytelling in a corporate culture is in the area of recruiting and attracting top talent. At Peppercomm, humor permeates our recruitment branding. For example, when we speak to candidates, our recruitment team will often share the uniqueness of our comedy training. This is internal storytelling, which our staff does every day for our clients and for ourselves. At that point, a light bulb goes off as the candidate realizes the connection between comedy and storytelling: it's so much more than just being funny.

Sierra Buck, account executive and coordinator of our Pep Squad summer internship program, has a clear perspective on how the next generation of talent makes this connection:

> In a way, everyone at Peppercomm is affected by Steve's unique sense of humor, and we share that general sensibility with our Pep Squad candidates. That plays well with college students looking to build a relationship with a New York PR firm that is "comedy-centric," if you will. At Peppercomm, we learn to develop our own individual comedy styles, so while we're all influenced in some way by Steve and Clayton, we also feel free to show our own personalities during the interview process. I find that, for me, making a joke during an interview about how I spilled coffee on my dress the first day I ever met my manager (true story, by the way) humanizes me and helps the person I'm interviewing to relax.
>
> We also get a good feel for whether candidates can walk the walk by asking them to show us why they want to be on the Pep Squad using various social media platforms. Some produce short videos that get right to the point and show us a bit of their personalities. They also show us their level of comfort with the various channels and the differences among them. These clips can serve to provide us with tremendous insight about who might fit in around here and who won't. This isn't to say it's a casting call where we only consider the most extroverted, but it allows us to see people's vulnerability, which is essential in our business. Most young people today are super accustomed to current

trends in social media content, and this part of the application process gives them a chance to share that side of themselves with us.

Even my own application to Peppercomm used technology. I created a special website using WordPress. On it, I provided screenshots of mock Instagram, Twitter, and LinkedIn posts, all encompassing why I wanted to be an intern at Peppercomm. Knowing how much the firm values comedy, I positioned my Instagram photo of myself all dressed in the go-to work attire of the day: professional from the waist up, pajama pants on the bottom. (This was during the COVID-19 lockdown. Nobody wore slacks back then.) I was holding brownies and a notebook entitled "The Four Levels of Comedy." I later heard that my self-deprecating photography showed an understanding of the corporate culture here and played a role in my being accepted to the Pep Squad program!

To this day, I try to do my part to encourage candidates to continue the tradition of using technology to show their personalities in the recruitment process.

Indeed, tailoring content with the sensibilities, sense of humor differences, and communication styles of different generations is a great way to break through to your target audience. Just like Sierra knows how to speak the language of today's college students, you must know how your audience communicates in order for your storytelling to shine through.

As Jennifer Murtell, vice president of strategy, Asia Pacific, at Marks, part of SGS & Co., writes in her article "Anticipating the Future of Generational Insights," "There is an inherent tension between customized brand experiences and universal, purpose-driven brand building. How can brands find their happy place, a resonant position in the landscape where every segment feels like the brand experience is uniquely designed for them?"[10]

It's a great question, and one answer lies in the shared language of comedy. Murtell continues, "In broad strokes, generations deal with unique cultural contexts, seismic economic shifts, civic and political realities, and rapidly evolving technology in totally different ways."

This disparity is reflected in their comedy preferences as well.

On a macro level, baby boomers tend to prefer clean material, jokes about current events, and wordplay. The Ford Transit Connect Wagon is a van designed specifically for this group, and their slogan? "The van for baby boomers whose idea of rocking doesn't involve a chair."[11]

Generation X came of age during a period of rebellious political incorrectness, so they generally prefer edgier comedy. In a brilliant ad by FTX starring Larry David as a founding father in 1776, in response to someone suggesting that people shall have the right to vote, Larry shouts, "Even the stupid ones?"[12]

Millennials' and Generation Z's comic sensibilities tend toward politically correct themes that reinforce their mostly progressive values. In a hilarious ad for Dunkin', Rapunzel has no use for the handsome prince who comes to rescue her.[13]

Developing an understanding of generational differences when it comes to comedy is necessary for any comedian who wants to get laughs from audiences of all ages. As it pertains to your brand's storytelling, it can be the difference between a yes and an "okay, boomer," with a roll of the eyes that would make your teenage daughter jealous.

Remember our trivago client we mentioned earlier? Here's another example of how a breakthrough success came from our applying our comedy training to come up with a totally unexpected punch line (well, it ended up being a pitch line to the media). Following the CEO's appearance on CNN, we had to keep the positive buzz going—despite the fact that almost all global travel was shut down due to COVID-19.

During our Peppercomm brainstorms, we're constantly prodding one another with unexpected questions to get our comedic juices flowing. A one-liner in one of our brainstorms became the platform for an entire campaign: With all of us stuck in lockdown, what would we give up to travel right now? We turned that question into an innovative survey of thousands of US consumers. And guess what? When we asked them what they would give up to travel, nearly 40 percent said sex![14] Media outlets went crazy for the data, landing trivago on every news desk from CNBC to Stephen Colbert.

* * * * * ROI TIP *from* STEVE * * * * * *

BEFORE OUR STORYTELLING plane takes off to the next destination on your readership sojourn, we would be remiss in not shouting out our public relations colleagues at Oatly (https://www.oatly.com/en-us). For those not in the know, Oatly is the world's original and largest oat drink company (an impressive credential to cite in anyone's CV).

Oatly demonstrated the power of humor in storytelling in a press release! We used the exclamation point since many public relations practitioners would gag if anyone suggested they use humor in a press release. The press release is sacrosanct in the wonderful world of PR and is considered an essential and serious component in any media relations tool kit. And woe betide the publicist who doesn't disseminate a press release that isn't short, succinct, and anything but funny.

That axiom holds true in many cases but is dead wrong when you're working for a brand that is attempting to outflank the competition, reach new audiences in unexpected ways, and, hold for it, craft a press release the press (read: reporters, editors, influencers, producers, the local fruit stand guy who's on a first-name basis with Nora O'Donnell, and so on) will not only read but publish! Go figure.

As you will see (and, hopefully, enjoy a hearty and much-needed guffaw), Oatly has taken a regional approach in its latest public relations campaign and, in order to heighten awareness within the greater Philadelphia market, issued a press release to introduce its new cream cheese with the following drop-dead funny (*and highly unexpected*) headline, dateline, and lead sentence:

Starting Today, Philadelphians Are Invited to Be the First to Experience the New Plant-Based Product, Now Available Exclusively at Spread Bagelry and Philly Bagels

Malmö, Sweden, and Philadelphia, Pennsylvania, Feb. 22, 2023—Oatly, the world's original and largest oat drink company, today announced the limited release of their new, forthcoming plant-based cream cheese, invented at the company's Philadelphia R&D lab. This groundbreaking innovation was spearheaded by Oatly's Philadelphia-based scientists, most of whom live in downtown Philadelphia, with the exception of a product developer who lives in Cherry Hill, New Jersey, but tells people he's "from five miles outside the city."

The rest of the press release is just as LOL funny.[15]

The news media loved it! Results included major coverage in food, regional, and business media.

Storytelling, both internal and external, must be vivid, honest, and equal parts funny and intriguing in order for your workplace to thrive and your external communications to produce results. At Peppercomm, we're always looking for opportunities to inject humor into our own press releases.

At the height of the pandemic, we decided it was time to play an April Fools' prank on the rest of the business world by introducing a new time-appropriate fashion statement for all the at-home remote workers living their lives on Zoom. Introducing, the Zoomsie, a two-part fashion statement that paired a button-down dress shirt with a comfy pair of sweatpants.[16] We were shocked that the business press took this ridiculous idea seriously, but it was a strange time.[17]

The publicity momentarily went to Steve's head, and he began to see himself as the Calvin Klein of COVID and contemplated opening a pop-up Zoomsie store in Times Square, but then he remembered the latter was empty.

TEAMWORK

In a healthy workplace culture, everyone in the company feels like part of the group. Everyone's opinions are respected, and everyone's contributions are valued. The evidence is clear that employees tend to resist change because there's no clear communication, shared purpose, and/or connectivity. "Providing an outlet for colleagues to share and see all the information related to a task, including progress updates and informal commentary, can create an important esprit de corps," concluded the researchers who worked on a 2015 McKinsey study entitled "Changing Change Management."[18] As Rupen Desai puts it, "None of us wants to live a life where we're facing hardships to make life better. And that's what most companies are asking us to do. We need ingenuity and unexpected solutions. That level of creativity can be learned by studying humor, laughter, and comedy."

Teamwork, connectivity, esprit de corps, whatever you like to call it, is the foundation of healthy relationships and success in the workplace. Peppercomm was acquired in 2021 by a phenomenal global agency called Ruder Finn (RF). So far, the marriage is going swimmingly. In 2022, RF decided to hold its first in-person employee retreat since the prepandemic days. They invited some 250 employees from around the United States, including our intrepid crew of fifty lost souls.

About a week after the event, the RF production company created a world-class, three-minute video that captured the highlights of the two-day retreat and included several lengthy interviews with employees.[19] For some reason, they chose to focus on a certain gregarious Peppercommer named Antonio who, truth be told, absolutely stole the show.

After the video was circulated to our employees, Steve simply had to break the silence by calling out Antonio on one of our weekly 12@12 meetings. "Wow, Antonio. The camera really loves you!" Immediately, the jokes started flying about our account manager's Oscar-worthy performance and whether he'd signed with Creative Artists Agency. Everyone contributed to a hilarious cavalcade of good-natured slings and arrows aimed at our matinee idol, Antonio "DiCaprio" DeSoto. To this day, whenever Antonio posts a notice that he needs to go to the dentist, is taking a day off, and so on, invariably someone posts a quip: "He's probably got an audition. I hear Spielberg is holding a casting call for the lead role in *E.T. 2*." Antonio, like any other A-list celebrity, basks in the adulation and enjoys the constant banter. It's a beautiful thing and a great example of how a comedy-infused culture leads to laughter in the workplace, which leads to happy employees.[20]

Speaking of happy employees, as of this writing, Peppercomm has managed to dodge the Great Resignation. Our voluntary turnover rate since March 2020 is an incredibly low *9 percent*! The national average was 56.8 percent in 2020 and 47.2 percent in 2021,[21] so this is one case in which we're happy to be well below average.

By the way, we remain in denial that we have ever had any turnover whatsoever. We're completely convinced that missing 9 percent simply got lost one day on their way to work. They are still part of our ongoing search-and-rescue efforts. That's client billable, right?

DM   **Danielle Montana**   3 months ago
Ruder Finn Group • News and Information Antonio DeSoto, our
star!!!! https://www.youtube.com/watch?v=nlvc Lz9jys

MD   **Marissa Dunn**   3 months ago
Antonio DeSoto you're a natural!

RM   **Rita McNeil**   3 months ago
Time to roll out the red carpet for him, yet again

MO   **Maggie ONeill**   3 months ago
Do they know he charges mode./SAG rates Has Peri
approved his contract? 😄

AD   **Antonio DeSoto**   3 months ago
Might be time for me to lawyer up, I haven't seen a dime
from RF yet 💰

BH   **Brianna Havraniak**   3 months ago
Antonio DeSoto make sure you're getting royalties from
that profound intellectual property

KC   **Kerri Callaghan**   3 months ago
Antonio DeSoto thank me and Caroline Mooney for your
claim to fame

AD   **Antonio DeSoto**   3 months ago
Tara do Keri, Caroline or Peppercomm have any claim to
a % of my royalties? Is there anything in the handbook on
that?

TL   **Tara Lillien**   3 months ago
You were terrific. Way to represent.

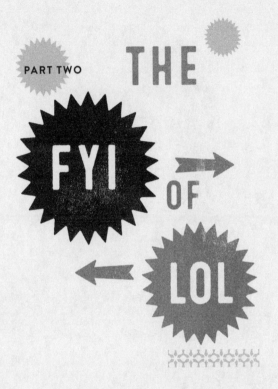

PART TWO

THE

FYI

OF

LOL

THREE DIFFERENT TYPES *of* COMEDY

STAND-UP COMEDY

ARE YOU KIDDING? Are we seriously going to learn about stand-up in a book about business? No, we're not kidding. In fact, we believe comedy is essential to the future of work. For those organizations that want to embrace the uncertainties in the workplace amid an ever-evolving business landscape, laughter is table stakes for survival.[1]

★ ★ ★ ★ ★ ★ **LOL TIP** *from* **CLAYTON** ★ ★ ★ ★ ★ ★

I'VE BEEN IN the performing arts throughout my life, and stand-up comedy is the only art form I've ever encountered that people think can't be taught. Perhaps because the best practitioners of it make it look so natural, some people think that you've either got this or you don't. I'm perplexed by this take, so let's explore it.

I have taught literally thousands of individuals the art of stand-up comedy through classes designed for actors who want a new skill to add to their résumés, corporate workshops designed for business leaders who want to do better at their jobs, and private coaching sessions with people from all walks of life who want to learn comedy for a wide range of reasons. Every single one of them got funnier, which proves that this stuff can, in fact, be taught.

Stand-up comedians are people who communicate effectively through laughter. We love watching Brian Regan, Ali Wong, Marina Franklin, or Gary Gulman share their thoughts and feelings in a way that makes us burst into hysterics. What these masters do is bring us into their worlds, indeed their very brains, and share what's inside. The result is a powerful connection that can't be achieved any other way. Performing solo, the stand-up takes the stage and shares stories, thoughts, and feelings to connect with and move an audience to laughter and much more.

Stand-up is an art form that begins with telling the truth. Long gone are the days of "three guys walk into a bar" with a contrived setup and predictable punch line. Today's stand-up is about authentic storytelling, which is what makes the skills practiced by today's masters of it so applicable to anyone who wants to be a better, more charismatic communicator.[2]

Charisma is an elusive trait, and one that is not easy to define. To borrow a turn of phrase from the late Supreme Court associate justice Potter Stewart (who was of course talking about obscenity at the time), "I don't know what it is, but I know it when I see it." Charisma is what makes it virtually impossible to take your eyes off a given performer. Whether it's Lady Gaga, Katt Williams, or Taylor Swift, some people just have the "it" factor, the power to attract and keep our attention from the moment they walk in. By developing your own charisma using the same techniques employed by these A-list performers, you can grab your audience's attention and achieve real bottom-line results in the process.

Sounds great, right? So how do we do it? Well, first off, bear in mind that charisma is mysterious and fluid. What works for one person may not work for another; so we're sorry, there's no magic potion here. But a team of management scholars led by John Antonakis of the University of Lausanne Business School in Switzerland certainly tried to brew one up. They conducted a study to answer the question "Can charisma be taught?" and determined that the answer is yes.[3] Anyone, yes, even you, can increase your personal charisma by doing one or more of the following:

- **Use metaphors.** Metaphors capture an audience's imagination.
- **Use stories and anecdotes.** People love to hear about your journey.
- **Show moral conviction.** Reinforcing shared ethical values builds trust.
- **Express shared feelings.** We all want to feel like someone feels the same way.
- **Set high expectations.** Let others know you believe in them.
- **Use contrasts.** Show everyone how different you are from the rest.
- **Use lists.** We have no idea what this means or why it builds charisma.

- **Use rhetorical questions.** Draw people in with guiding language.
- **Animate your words.** Body language, facial expressions, and tonality hook them in.

Comedians learn to develop charisma by applying these techniques on a nightly basis and finding out *through trial and error* what works most consistently for them. The goal is to become undeniably engaging, to be the person every audience finds interesting, compelling, and impossible to forget.

KEY SKILLS OF STAND-UP COMEDY

Great stand-up comedians know how to connect with vastly diverse audiences. The key skills that enable their charisma to heighten the effects of their performances are vulnerability, emotional fullness, and sensitivity. In this section, we'll examine each of these skills individually.

Vulnerability

Telling the truth isn't always easy. We all want to be loved, and you might think that the road to that end is paved with presenting yourself in the best possible light. On the contrary, stand-ups know that the opposite best resonates with audiences. As soon as you go onstage and say, "I have a problem," you connect with everyone in the audience in a real and genuine way. No one can relate to "I have a mansion and a yacht and a perfect life at home." Comics know this and use what's wrong as the place to start rather than something to hide. By admitting that she doesn't have all the answers or is otherwise imperfect, the stand-up comic endears herself to the audience because we see ourselves in her vulnerability. She's relatable and now we all want to be her friends.

Emotional Fullness

Stand-up comedians are engaging, passionate, compelling performers. One key factor in this is their willingness to allow their emotions to come out. By bringing their whole selves to the stage, comedians are able to communicate and connect in a real and vulnerable way. Sharing emotion is not a sign of weakness but rather strength. We love watching stand-ups "go for it" with high levels of emotion because it's almost like watching a high-wire act. The risk the performer is taking by sharing this emotional roller coaster is actually what makes the comic compelling and bonds the audience to the performance. As Maya Angelou so eloquently said, "People will forget what you said, people will forget what you did, but people will never forget how you made them feel."

When performing stand-up, there should be present a certain fear factor. The comedian is being honest and conveying his true emotions. He's allowing himself to be judged, baring virtually all for the audience to like, hate, admire, disparage, or resent. When the great Gary Gulman shares his thoughts on basketball, he's actually revealing his truth about himself.[4]

So, I was big. I was big, and I was sensitive and soft, growing up. And when you were big, back then, you were encouraged/harassed into playing sports.

And I—I didn't want to play the footballs, the hockeys, the contact sports, that was not for me. I fell in love with basketball almost immediately, because basketball just fits my personality. It still does. Basketball is the only sport you can practice by yourself.

I spent a lot of time practicing basketball by myself, and basketball also fits maybe because it's the only sport where if somebody so much as slaps you on the wrist, they stop the game. Stop the game, separate everyone, and let you make two easy shots while everyone else is forced to watch quietly, as if to say, "Think about what you did."

And I was automatic from the free-throw line, because free-throw shooting is a direct function of childhood loneliness. I have this carnival skill. If you tell me you were a good high school free-throw shooter, you can give me your high school free-throw shooting percentage, and I can tell you what time your single mother got home from work. I shot 94 percent my senior year. My mother was a night court bailiff.

When to Say When

Gary is a master of tension and release. He builds the former with truthful material designed to make us feel something for him. He releases that tension with the laughter, reminding us that he's okay after all. Comedians must observe and sense audiences to figure out where exactly that line is. How much would be too much for this particular group of people? What one audience would consider the perfect dose of reality another would call TMI. It's up to the performer to read the room and be willing to change course midperformance to take the audience on a trip they actually want to take.

Sensitivity

The first question an experienced stand-up will ask the emcee upon arrival at a comedy club is, "How's the crowd?" Answers to this question can range from uptight to up-for-anything. The reason this question matters is that a great performance is actually tailored to the crowd. Every stand-up performance is unique and designed to some degree with the whims and desires of tonight's audience in mind. The uptight 7:00 p.m. after-work crowd on a Wednesday will not enjoy the same material as the rowdy and raucous midnight Saturday bunch. It would be a huge mistake for the comic to neglect, and fail to adapt to, the different sensibilities of different audiences.

Crossing the Line

Being sensitive also enables you to see potential pitfalls before arriving at them. We believe that no one takes the stage with the intention of offending the audience, and yet it happens all the time. A lack of sensitivity, or an inability to read the crowd and make real-time decisions on what material to avoid, has been the downfall of many performers since the beginning of time. Think Michael Richards, Daniel Tosh, and Roseanne Barr for context here, and Google them at your own risk.

Whenever we first introduce the idea of learning stand-up comedy at work, we know that we should plug our ears to fight the screams of horror that follow from the voice boxes of the HR department heads we're addressing. There is a widespread misconception about stand-up: that it must be raunchy, dirty, irreverent, vulgar, politically incorrect, and controversial. In fairness, much stand-up is like that! But your best Nikki Glaser impression isn't going to fly in the conference room, so we take measures to quell the understandable fear the human resource manager experiences. First, we show examples from our own comedy material that are clean, funny, and business appropriate. Next, we acknowledge that every corporate culture is different, and that part of the assignment is to know where the line we don't cross is. Finally, we love to borrow a phrase from the New York City Department of Sanitation. In their early posters designed to help people learn how and what to recycle, they made the point that anything you're not sure can be recycled should be discarded with the regular trash: "When in Doubt, Leave It Out."

Changing the GPS

Sensitivity also applies to the relationship between performer and audience. The best stand-ups are able to make midcourse corrections based on the feedback they're getting (or not getting) from an audience. This could include abandoning a particular joke altogether, or possibly even going to a whole separate batch of material that is designed to fix the bad vibes in the room. Doing so humanizes the performer and rewards the fact that he addressed the elephant in the room with the audience's sympathy. (By the way, how *did* that elephant get in the room anyway?) Being fair and honest about how poorly a performance is going can often win over an audience who had previously dialed you out.

★ ★ ★ ★ ★ ★ LOL TIP *from* CLAYTON ★ ★ ★ ★ ★ ★

A HUGE LESSON that my twenty-plus years of performing on the world's comedy stages has taught me is the value of failure. Believe me, it hurts me to the core every single time an audience doesn't immediately take to me, but there's a silver lining. In those moments of desperately seeking and not receiving love from a room full of strangers, I learn things about myself. Turns out, I do some of my best thinking when the fight-or-flight response kicks in, which it does whenever I'm bombing. In this state, I'm able to access my most resilient, creative brain cells because it literally feels like I'm dying! The body responds with a form of overdrive, and what may have come out as panic in my early performing days now comes out as what comics call a "save."

I have more than thirty minutes of bombing material, jokes about how it's not going well. "Wow, when you guys get quiet, you do it as a group. You're all on the same page; if one person thinks it's not funny, it's unanimous. Most audiences laugh and clap a lot; you guys are a nice change of pace." These punch lines were all born in real time as improvised offhand comments. They serve to get laughs while letting audiences know that I'm fine, as I'm clearly coping. But more important, they offer me the opportunity to save the set. Maybe if people can see me as a human being, they'll give my material another chance.

An essential component of any creative endeavor is failure. The process of developing a powerhouse stand-up comedy set involves copious amounts of trial, error, error, error, and back to the drawing board. Revising material, trying different delivery styles, and experimenting with an open mind eventually leads to the gold the comic is seeking. As Oprah Winfrey once said, "Failure is another stepping stone to greatness."

FORMS OF STAND-UP COMEDY

Stand-up comes in many forms including observational, anecdotal, put-down, blue (speakers of the unspeakable), musical, prop, and alternative comedy. For this book, we'll focus on observational, anecdotal, and put-down comedy because they all have direct and meaningful business applications. In this section, we'll examine these three forms from an artistic standpoint and get to the business applications later.

Observational

Observational comedy, as practiced by Ali Wong and Jerry Seinfeld, takes us inside the mind of the comic, who shares thoughts and feelings on a particular subject. We learn that no two people see life through the same set of eyes, and we laugh hysterically at the commentary.

Observational stand-up is a dialogue between the performer and the audience in which the audience only says ha. It's up to the comic to decipher what each ha means, based on the tone and volume of the laughs but also the nonverbal communication that accompanies each one. Does the laugh imply agreement, horror, disapproval, resonance, dissonance, or something else? A great comedian knows which buttons to press and when in order to take the audience on a fantastic journey through the inner workings of his mind. Emotional fullness is the key here: the subject matters less than the comic's *feelings* on the subject, as a human being's truth is revealed in unexpected and hilarious ways.

Clayton has his own views on living life as a color-blind person:

I'm color-blind. So when people learn this about me, the first thing they say is, "Oh, you're color-blind? What color is this?" I just told you I'm color-blind. You don't go up to blind people and say, "How many fingers am I holding up?" Would you ask a deaf guy, "Can you hear me now?" But the best are the people who try to teach me. They're like, "This is red and this is green." I say, "I'm cured! Hey, nobody ever explained it like that before. Where have you been all my life? That's red and that's green. Problem solved!" I'm color-blind, not color-stupid!

One time another comic told me, "Wow, Clayton. The audience loved your color-blind jokes. You're lucky because you've got something wrong with you. I just wish I had something wrong with me." I said, "If you think about it, you've got something wrong with you too. You're completely tactless, Carrot Top." I still don't like that guy. I don't know what color his hair is, but I am not a fan.

Many participants in our ongoing stand-up workshops use the observational form when they try comedy for the first time. Often, it will be a universally shared complaint about the organization's abysmal IT infrastructure. Or they'll poke fun at someone in the upper echelon who insists weekly reports be in his inbox no later than 3:47 p.m. every Friday (no one knows if the titan even reads them since it's always radio silence the following Monday). Other times, they'll call out a particular quirk of one of their colleagues in the room where we're holding the training.

One woman at a session we did for a pharmaceutical client noted in her stand-up routine that "Jimmy" always seems distracted on Zoom meetings. She stopped, looked over at Jimmy, and said, "Hey, he's even distracted in live meetings. The bastard's multitasking while I'm up here desperately trying to be funny. Thanks, Jimmy. Remind me to ignore you on tomorrow's call." Everyone laughed, including an embarrassed Jimbo, who put down his mobile device and was extremely attentive for the rest of the session.

Anecdotal

Anecdotal comedy, as practiced by Ronnie Chieng and Kevin Hart, is storytelling with punch lines. The performer shares true (or mostly true) tales from his life, and the audience comes along for the ride, rooting for the hero (or antihero) doing the speaking.

Anecdotal stand-up brings the audience closer to the performer due to the natural emotional investment associated with hearing about another person's struggles, fears, or obstacles. Indeed, the best comedy stories come from situations in which the performer is the underdog, a fish out of water, or a stranger in a strange land who has a mountain to climb. Everyone loves an underdog, and the audience roots for Ronnie to figure out how to explain American life to his Asian parents or for Kevin to get revenge on his bullies. We love stars who are willing to share their insecurities, short-comings, and truths for comic effect.

Bonnie McFarlane, veteran comic and host of the *My Wife Hates Me* podcast, shares an underdog story filled with insecurities and shortcomings about the time her house burned down on Comedy Central's *This Is Not Happening.*[5] In the piece, McFarlane wins the audience over by truth-fully sharing not only the events of that fateful day but also her feelings about herself as a parent whose daughter was in danger. In a vulnerable and hilarious way, McFarlane brings this story of a five-alarm fire to life.

The key to anecdotal comedy is to keep the audience in-trigued throughout your story with as many twists, turns, and punch lines as possible. The audience expects to laugh throughout the narrative, not just at the end, and in hearing Bonnie McFarlane's fiery tale, they do.

Put-Down

Put-down comedy, as practiced by Joan Rivers and Patrice O'Neal, is poking fun at other people for comic effect. In-sulting everything from people's fashion choices to their political viewpoints, stand-ups take the liberty to be mean in the spirit of good fun.

This style of stand-up depends on buy-in from both the audience and the person being insulted, if present. Typ-ically, the audience agrees that the person being torn to shreds deserves it for some reason. Punching up, attacking those with status, money, fame, or power, is key to pulling this risky style of comedy off. Roasting Justin Bieber at the Friars Club is actually a form of affection. When put-down humor goes well, it's because everyone's in on the joke, including its target. When it doesn't go well, it's usually because it's too mean-spirited or the boss isn't laughing!

* * * * * * **LOL TIP *from* CLAYTON** * * * * * *

EVERY YEAR, right before the holidays, Peppercomm puts together a charity fundraiser at a New York City comedy club. The "gimmick" for this special show is that you're going to see a group of businesspeople from Peppercomm all making their NYC stand-up comedy debuts, and all in the name of charity. I'll be performing, too, of course, but I'm not the big draw on this night. The employee "debutantes" are.

Our public relations and digital marketing account supervisors, our information technology specialists, and even our interns get to perform material they've been working on with me as part of our regular, ongoing in-house comedy training. But this time, the stakes are higher than ever. It's one thing to bounce joke ideas off the chief comedy officer in a poorly lit conference room during normal work hours, but this is different. Tonight, they'll be on an actual NYC stage in front of a sold-out studio audience!

I relish the opportunity to help prepare these debut performers for their big night and love seeing their reactions after, one by one, they "kill." I especially enjoy seeing the delighted expressions on the faces of their assembled families, friends, colleagues, and clients. Proceeds from the event benefit a worthy cause chosen by our employees, and the feeling in the room that night is never anything short of blissful. Who doesn't want to contribute to a worthy cause and share a few laughs along the way?

In contrast to all these warm and fuzzies, a running gag at these events is the annual vicious obliteration of our beloved chief executive officer, Mr. Steven Cody. Steve, serving as your host for the evening, introduces each "comedian" with a warm and loving setup such as, "Our next performer is not only hilarious, she's also one of my closest friends of twenty years and I'd be nothing without her. Please welcome to the stage my dear friend and Peppercomm's executive vice president, Jackie Kolek!" Jackie's opening line stands in contrast to all that sentimentality: "Thanks, Steve. Your jacket doesn't fit and your material sucks." The audience is delighted watching comic after comic knock the boss down a few pegs, and Steve loves all kinds of attention, so naturally he eats up the barbs as well.

Working on this show is the highlight of my year, every year.

It should be noted that many stand-up performers weave in and out of the different forms. For example, you might use observational style to talk about the Waze app on your phone within an anecdotal piece about a road trip you once took with your family. Perhaps while observing something people do that you despise, you might decide to disparage someone you know who is guilty of doing that exact thing using the put-down form. It's not necessary to choose just one style and stick to it, but you should know what form you're using at all times.

STAND-UP COMEDY TECHNIQUES

Comics have so many tricks up their sleeves to make us laugh. The best comedians know which trick to use and when. Let's break down the different techniques of writing and performing stand-up comedy.

Nerves

If the idea of standing in front of a room filled with your coworkers and telling a funny story makes you feel a little queasy, good! That queasiness is incontrovertible proof that you're a living, breathing human being. It's natural to be nervous before a performance.

Think of all the times in your life when you felt those little butterflies in your stomach. Maybe it was the day you asked her to marry you. The day you took the SAT hoping not to have to enroll in your safety school. The day you interviewed for the job you have now. The first time you went skydiving or climbed Mount Washington (what are you, crazy?). The common thread of all these important life moments is that the outcome mattered greatly to you.

Nerves are your friend onstage. The fact that you are nervous conveys to the audience that you care about the performance, it means something to you, and you're definitely not phoning it in. Interestingly, the audience does not see a quivering leaf or delicate flower shaking in the breeze. The nerves always come out as excitement, enthusiasm for the story or thought being shared.

There are two kinds of energy, potential and kinetic. When nervous energy is bottled up inside, it feels like sweaty palms or those damn butterflies (when is migration season anyway?) because the energy is trying to go somewhere. It's potential energy, not unlike the taut rubber bands of a sling-shot about to be fired. Once it's released as the emcee says, "And now, coming to the stage," it becomes kinetic energy that must now be focused. Performers learn how to use their nervousness as a kind of turbo booster to give a performance the weight it deserves. Like the black swan in the Darren Aronofsky masterpiece of the same name, the performer lets go of all nervousness, self-doubt, and introversion, allowing herself to soar to heights she could never reach without the presence of those wonderful, pesky butterflies.

Channel your nervous energy into excitement, commitment, and emotional fullness and you will breathe so much life into your performance, Natalie Portman will ask to borrow your wings.

Setups and Punch Lines

All stand-up material can be broken down into setups and punch lines. The punch line, as you probably know, is the part that gets the laugh. A great punch line is short, surprising, and shows a shift in attitude. Someone once said that comedy is pretending I'm going to give you this, but I give you that instead.

A setup reveals your subject and how you feel about your subject. Remember that emotional fullness is key to developing charisma, so don't forget to share your feelings.

Let's look at a classic Henny Youngman example from the late 1950s. For context, remember that this was the precursor to what later became known as the Women's Liberation Movement, a period during which women were joining the workforce in great numbers, changing the landscape of the America we once knew. Youngman commented, "Women's role in society is really changing; take my wife. Please!" The setup is the subject, women joining the workforce, and how he feels, optimistic. The punch line, "Please," is short, one syllable. It also catches us by surprise and shows a shift in attitude from optimism to desperation.

Youngman and his contemporaries paved the way for today's comedy writers, who know the best way to get a big laugh is to say something the audience couldn't see coming from a mile away. As the multitalented comedy actor/writer/director Jordan Peele puts it, "I'm obsessed with giving the audience something they don't see coming."

* * * * * * **LOL TIP** *from* **CLAYTON** * * * * * *

I HAVE LEARNED in my career that the best punch lines are vivid and specific. In addition to surprising the audience, we need to paint a clear picture for them with our word choices, inflections, and body language. We see this concept in action in a segment from my 2023 comedy special, *Middle Child Syndrome*:

My six-year-old daughter's a genius; she got into a highly selective elementary school for brilliant kids. I always knew, though. Last winter, we were walking in Central Park, and I said, "Honey, I think I just saw a ladybug." She frowned, "No you didn't. Come on, Daddy. Ladybugs hibernate. Didn't you know that? And also, they're not indigenous to the

Northeast quadrant of the park." I said, "Go to your room." I'm joking—she's not going anywhere; she's teaching me chess. She can't go to her room until I learn the Latvian Gambit.

This material gets laughs partly because of the mental images painted by the carefully worded punch lines. My goal is to have the audience feel like they're taking that walk in the park with us, coming along for the ride. I only hope they don't end up feeling as dumb as I did that day in the park.

Roll Structure

You've heard people say, "Don't stop now, you're on a roll," or "She really had them rolling." With all due respect to anyone who's ever played craps, this term came from the comedy world first. A roll is a writing style in which there are multiple punch lines per setup. Examples include Bill Maher's "New Rules" or Jeff Foxworthy's "You might be a redneck" trope. Most modern stand-up is in this format.

The reason why roll structure is so powerful is that the audience has bought into the comic premise and is now enjoying the ride. We need not veer away from the thesis because they're "with" us. (Does thesis rhyme with "with us"? We'll take the points.) We're enjoying these surprises together, and everyone gets the point. By making our feelings known in this way, we offer the audience the opportunity to absorb the evidence as we build our case. It's a more effective method of oral communication than bombarding them with facts, figures, charts, graphs, and pretty PowerPoint slides. And it sure beats rinsing and repeating.

★ ★ ★ ★ ★ ★ LOL TIP *from* CLAYTON ★ ★ ★ ★ ★ ★

AT LEAST 90 PERCENT of all professional stand-up comedy is written in roll structure. When I get an audience laughing, I like to keep them laughing, and that's what getting on a roll is all about. On the aforementioned *Middle Child Syndrome*, I have a roll about how I feel the traditional wedding invitation template doesn't include enough boxes for the invitee to choose from:

"There's 'Graciously Accepts' or 'Regretfully Declines.' They should have 'Regretfully Accepts.' Yes, I'm very sorry to tell you, I'll be at your wedding. I'm going but I really wish I didn't have to. I'll have the chicken. Or how about 'Cheerfully Declines'? Be honest, have you ever gotten an invite and you wanted to say, 'Not going, don't care, screw you!' How about a 'Screw You' box? How about 'You Didn't Come to Our Wedding So Go Suck an Egg!' How about 'We Never Liked You, How'd You Get This Address?' We need an 'Unsubscribe' box for sure. Take me off your list!"

Comedians like to say there's more juice left in the orange, meaning a comic idea has not been fully developed. There are some more laughs in there, so keep on squeezing.

Act Out

"Show me, don't tell me," read the lyrics to the song of the same title by Canadian rock powerband Rush on their 1989 double-platinum album, *Presto*. This song also includes the lyric "Let's try to keep it short." Both lyrics are excellent advice for stand-up comedians.

The act-out technique involves demonstrating, rather than mentioning, someone. Show me, don't tell me, whatever it is you're trying to share about that person. It could be a famous person we all know imitated in lifelike perfection (impersonation technique). More often, though, the comedian acts someone out that the audience doesn't know. A man on the street who approached me, the cashier at Starbucks, someone who works in the research department, my spouse, or anyone else in my story.

The comic changes her voice, mannerisms, body language, and so on to demonstrate those of another character in the "scene" she's sharing. The act out is also a great way to show (don't tell) how you felt in a given moment: "I was like, 'Wow, nobody ever explained it like that before! Thanks for pointing that out to me!' as though I'd never thought of that myself." Acting yourself out, going back in time and reliving a moment you experienced, is a great way to share a story with bonus material, the director's commentary.

The reason this technique is so effective is that it raises the stakes for you and for the audience. Rather than passively talking about whatever your subject happens to be, you're actively living in the emotions that the subject makes you feel. Audiences love to see a performer take that leap into another time and place and trust them to come along for the ride. Really "going for it" in an act out is inherently riskier than telling a story in a third-person detached voice, and the rewards are proportionately great. By putting yourself into the scene you're setting, you build trust with an audience by raising the stakes for you and for them.

In his Tony-nominated one-man Broadway show *Freak,* the infinitely charismatic comedian John Leguizamo plays no fewer than twenty-three characters! Importantly, in between these act outs, Leguizamo addresses the audience directly, in real-time present tense. This ability to live in the moment and relive past moments is an indicator of the star performer's undeniable talent.

We're not expecting your senior vice president of marketing to suddenly become John Leguizamo; and to be clear, he doesn't have to. Audiences don't actually expect incredible acting or impersonation skills from comedians. In many ways, if the other person is impersonated badly, with over-the-top exaggeration, it ends up being funnier than if the impression were actually spot-on perfect. Don't worry if your accent is a bit off or the voice sounds a little squeaky; the more imperfect, the better! With a bit of practice, anyone can learn and apply this important technique to add life and color to his stand-up comedy material.

If you're ever struggling with exactly how to deliver a particular message in a powerful way, just remember the lyrics as sung by our favorite bassist, Geddy Lee, and "Show me, don't tell me."

Callbacks

You may have noticed that the name Elon Musk has already come up within this text. By repeatedly referencing our favorite Silicon Valley bad boy, we're practicing what comedians know as the callback technique.

A callback is when the performer brings up a subject that has already been mentioned, either by herself, one of the other performers, or perhaps even a member of the comedy club audience. The audience laughs instinctively at the mere mention of the aforementioned because they feel like they get the joke. It's an inside joke, of the moment and anything but rote, and the audience is on the inside. The callback is such a powerful tool that many comedians will end a long set with a well-chosen callback, essentially putting the final bow on an already beautiful package.

STAND-UP COMEDY STEP-BY-STEP

You might be thinking, "This is all well and good, guys, but how exactly does it work?" Well, fine. We'll give you a taste of the secret sauce.

An introductory stand-up comedy training session usually lasts about three hours. We start off with a short lecture on some of the key concepts shared in this chapter. Basic skills are explored and demonstrated by the two of us. The atmosphere is typically nervous and trepidatious. We like it that way because we know what's coming.

The next thing we do is ask everyone in the room to grab pencil and paper for a brainstorm. The prompt: Assuming you're called upon to take the stage, what will you say and how will you say it? If the vibe in the room was nervous before, it's borderline cardiac arrest now! Not to worry, though. We have a guided brainstorm designed to help every single attendee come up with at least one potential premise for an improvised stand-up comedy routine. During the brainstorm, we circle the room, helping everyone with the writing exercise and encouraging some to volunteer.

By now, most people need a break, so let's take five (okay, ten) and when we come back, the room always feels energized. There's just something electric about anticipation, and you can always feel it at this point in the session. Some people are excited to share what they came up with; others are absolutely mortified at the prospect. Everyone is as nervous as can be.

Next, to everyone's delight, the most senior executive in the room volunteers to give this exercise—far outside anyone's comfort zone—a go! Cheers erupt and the executive takes the microphone. A minute or two later, she is getting real-time feedback from the two of us on areas such as clarity, timing, presentation, body language, relatability, vulnerability, and so on. We each point out a few highlights we particularly enjoyed about the performance and then ask for another volunteer.

Hands shoot up and, one by one, all the attendees try stand-up comedy for the first time ever, in front of their coworkers. Each performer gets copious encouragement from us and, more important, from each other.

At the end of the session, we talk about how to use the skills learned to change the way business is conducted back at the office the next day. We also talk about how the feeling in the room evolved throughout the session and what that shift means. Then we talk about the real team building that has occurred as colleagues have shared their truths and about a million laughs with one another in the room.

A session like this one is the introduction to an ongoing program of comedy classes that we prescribe with the needs of the individual organization in mind. It all starts with laughter; where it goes from there is up to you.

KEY TAKEAWAYS

- **Authenticity**

  Begin with the truth, feel free to exaggerate within the boundaries of your culture.

  Use vulnerability and emotional fullness to connect.

  Don't worry about being funny at first; just be genuine.

- **Engagement**

  Be in the room; break the fourth wall.

  Listen and react to your audience's responses.

  Bring moments and feelings to life through demonstration.

- **Sensitivity**

  Read the room; know what is or isn't working and adjust accordingly.

  Make educated guesses on what an audience will or won't appreciate.

  When in doubt, leave it out.

6

IMPROVISATIONAL COMEDY

IMPROVISATIONAL COMEDY, or improv, is the creative process used in comedic content development of all forms. Even stand-up begins as improvised speech around a particular subject, and when it's done correctly, it still feels like the speaker is just "riffing." TV shows like *Whose Line Is It Anyway* and *Wild 'N Out* feature content that is purely improvised and never edited, revised, or refined. Other programs such as *Curb Your Enthusiasm* are unscripted but structured, meaning the characters and plot are prewritten, but the actual spoken lines are mostly improvised. All of these shows feature experienced improvisers who seemingly create comedy magic out of thin air.

You may wonder how a person can learn to improvise and why someone in the business world would even want to. There are fundamental skills that the best improvisers all have mastered and that we think everyone in business should learn, too, including:

- How to listen and observe actively and effectively

- How to be truthful and compelling in storytelling
- How to stimulate innovative and creative thinking

The best improv teams (or troupes, as they are sometimes called) know the nuts and bolts of working as a unit to develop a story. They practice ad libitum storytelling techniques so often that finding a beginning, middle, and end as a team becomes second nature to them. Every improv exercise (or game, as we call them) has a goal, be it using five predetermined words, reaching a coherent ending, making up a song in under five minutes, and so on.

KEY SKILLS OF IMPROVISATIONAL COMEDY

Just like with stand-up, the world of improv has its own set of skills: acceptance, building, and teamwork. These skills are learned individually through the various games until incorporating them becomes second nature to the performers practicing the art. It doesn't happen overnight but through practice and intentional repetition. Just as no golfer ever gets a hole-in-one the first time holding a club, even the most talented and dynamic performer can't master the art of improvisation without lots of practice.

Acceptance

In improv, we say that the first idea is the best idea. With tremendous enthusiasm and openness, we accept our scene partner's opening line as something to be treated as a given for the remainder of the exercise. When the first word in your scene partner's mind is always *yes*, you feel free to explore and experiment. Because improv groups have faith in one another, they know that everyone is paddling the boat in the same direction and that land will eventually be hoed (wait, we don't think that's quite right).

It takes a lot of practice and experience to learn how to open one's mind to suggestion in this way. The natural tendency, particularly among "alpha" types, is to try to control the situation, grabbing the bull by the horns. It can be scary to give someone else the power to guide the story, and many of us struggle in the beginning to rid ourselves of our own preconceived notions about how a scene should go. It's a fundamental skill, though, and critical to anyone who wants to be a great improviser.

We particularly enjoy a certain scene from Comedy Central's *Whose Line Is It Anyway*. In it, three world-class improv performers accept each other's spoken and physical choices to keep the scene moving and drive the action, regardless of how hectic.[1] By following another actor's lead in real time rather than trying to drive the action himself, each of these masters contributes to a chaotic and hilarious team performance.

Acceptance starts with yes.

Building

Building is the act of adding on to the story in progress. It starts with listening and accepting the premise of the scene. Skillful improv performers are able to take the comic idea and add on to it with the overall objective of the game front of mind at all times.

We work with companies regularly who've had less than stellar results trying to apply what they learn in improv games to their corporate lives. Often, the complaint is that the games feel silly, that the business executive trying to play them simply isn't comfortable portraying a frog in the grass in front of direct reports and colleagues. To be fair, because of the volatile and unpredictable nature of improv, some scenes do take quite ridiculous and silly turns. Not all businesspeople are comfortable with going with the flow in that way, and not all corporate cultures lend themselves to such experimentation. We respect that. Rather than trying to turn a frog into a prince (that is, a conservative and buttoned-up group into a carefree and uninhibited room full of Will Ferrells), we focus on storytelling games anyone should find firmly within their comfort zone.

One such game is the most basic improv exercise of all, the "yes, and . . ." game. The rules are simple: try to tell a coherent story one sentence (and one player) at a time using acceptance and building. We ask the participants to start off in a circle and begin with a prompt such as "I can't wait to get to the zoo!" The goal is to compose a group narrative something like this:

ANNIE: I can't wait to get to the zoo.

JAMARR: Yes, and we'd better hurry. It closes at four o'clock.

BONNIE: Yes, and there's a great new gorilla exhibit I don't want to miss.

LUCAS: Yes, and we can carpool so we can take the HOV lane!

MARIA: Yes, and the HOV lane will get us there by three o'clock.

RAY: Yes, and that's plenty of time to see the gorillas!

So, rather than a scene wherein your senior vice president of finance has to jump up and down like a gorilla in the zoo, we have an improvised story that involves acceptance and building. We'll get the VP into a gorilla suit in the advanced course.

Teamwork

Great improv teams are always trying to put their heads together to solve the puzzle of finding an ending for a scene that makes sense. Because there is no script, each "actor" must rely on the others onstage to accomplish the common goal. To that end, we recommend a mindset of trying to make the other performers look like stars.

If you're working on an improv scene and you're trying to be the loudest, funniest, and most interesting, there's a great chance that you're not leaving much room for your teammates to shine. While you're chewing up the scenery, the scene is suffering, and the goal is nowhere in sight. Teamwork means leading the league in assists, not points.

By accepting, building, and working as a unit, you and your team can learn to think faster on your feet. (Where the heck does that expression come from anyway? Of course I'm standing on my feet. No, let me think faster on my rib cage.) You can learn to trust each other to throw away the script and ad-lib like the pros.

FORMS OF IMPROVISATIONAL COMEDY

Short-Form Improv

Short-form improv consists of quick exercises, games designed to teach or emphasize a particular skill such as

listening, teamwork, or building. The actors create spontaneous comedy with the help of preset scenarios within the
framework of the object of the particular game being played.
Television programs like the aforementioned *Wild 'N Out*
and *Whose Line Is It Anyway?* are actual competitions, game
shows in which teams win points based on how well they
play the games.

Short-form improv games are fun to play and are perfect
for isolating a particular skill and drilling the fundamentals
home. We already talked about one such game, the "yes,
and . . ." game, which is the basic foundation of all improv.
Another is the "One-Word Story" game, in which teams
learn listening skills by building a narrative with a coherent
beginning, middle, and end with each participant limited
to only one word at a time.[2] There are hundreds of these
games, and the more you play them, the better your overall
improvisational comedy skills become.

Long-Form Improv

Long-form improv involves building an actual scene using
the various skills acquired through the short-form improv
games. Long-form improv relies not on a preset construct
but rather on the skills and talents of the troupe members
to build and finish a complete scene with one central idea
(the first one; that is, the best one). A well-performed long-
form scene closely resembles a complete scripted comedy
sketch, but the action and dialogue are not scripted at all
but improvised.

This form of improv comedy requires a tremendous
amount of teamwork to pull off. Listening, accepting, building, and concluding can happen only if all participants
work together. Even one team member pushing things in

the opposite direction can cause everything to break down to the point where the entire unit is unable to achieve the goal of building and finishing a complete scene.

Jackie Kolek, one of our senior leaders, takes an annual two-week vacation to Block Island, a tiny oasis off the coast of Rhode Island. During her trip one year, we were invited to pitch a major insurance company in Hartford, Connecticut, requiring Kolek, who happens to be our resident insurance expert, to join us for the pitch.

We started the pitch by introducing ourselves. When it was Jackie's turn, she said, "I just flew in here from my vacation on a tiny, eight-seater plane. Please don't let the fact that I risked my life to be here factor into your decision." The room immediately erupted into laughter, and we were awarded the business shortly thereafter.

By learning the skills of long-form improv, you will gain the confidence to trust your own storytelling abilities and make it up as you go along.

Harold Scenes

The crème de la crème of the improv genre is the Harold. A Harold begins with a prompt, often a single word. The prompt inspires a collection of scenes that make up a complete piece, similar to a three-act play with a set structure. Each scene is revisited and improvised twice more with the intention of connecting the three in a natural, organic, and surprising way. If you've ever noticed how the plot and subplots of virtually every *Seinfeld* episode intertwine, now you know why. That brilliant show's creators had their equally brilliant actors turn every germ of a premise into a full Harold, and the best ones eventually became the scripts of one of the funniest television series of all time.

Of course, acquiring the skills necessary to perform a successful Harold takes years of time, energy, and dedication. We're not suggesting that your company has to eventually become adept at building an improvised three-act play, of course! But understanding the structure and concept of the form can help drive your company's internal and external storytelling to new heights of creativity, clarity, and engagement.

TOOLS OF IMPROV

The "First-Best" Rule

Improv teams create magical moments in real time before a live audience. They don't have time to argue about, or debate, the pros and cons of this idea or that suggestion. In order for spontaneous scene creation to occur, the team must agree on one idea, and that idea is the first one presented. This is called the "First-Best" Rule of Improvisation. No matter how ludicrous, unexpected, or different from what one actor originally had in mind, the first idea is the one we're going with! This is powerful because it eliminates the game of tug-of-war that would otherwise typically ensue.

The Positivity Rule

In order for the action of a scene to build, flow, and advance, the characters in it need to want to be there. Think of a stereotypical on-set prima donna asking her director, "What's my motivation, dahling?" In improv, your motivation has to be a common goal with your scene partners. What are we trying to accomplish? The Positivity Rule states that beginning with abundance and optimism raises the ceiling on where the scene can potentially travel. Imagine a scene is about a vacation wherein some characters are lamenting not having money to afford travel and others are unable to get the PTO required to join the trip. That scene's going nowhere. Now imagine the same scene, but this time, the sky's the limit. Now we have characters who are talking about exciting adventures with fascinating people in exotic locations and action can move forward. Negativity and deprivation are absolute scene killers and must be avoided.[3]

Bold Choices

The best improvised scenes feature fearless actors taking big risks and giant leaps of faith, trusting both their teammates and the audience to follow them wherever they go. If everyone is timid due to inhibitions, fear of messing up, or other insecurities, the scene is likely to be boring and safe. Bold choices are a hallmark of strong improv.

In a classic scene from *Wild 'N Out,* the hilarious Maddy Smith showed tremendous bravery in displaying her less-than-impressive dance skills.[4]

Audiences love seeing a performer take that risk, but the other side of the coin is that the performer trusts (a) the audience and (b) the other performers to *accept* the risk she takes in making such a strong choice and run with it. Don't ask permission; don't be timid. In improv, you just have to go for it!

Statements, Not Questions

A good improviser knows how to make bold choices and take responsibility for pushing a scene forward. With few exceptions, this means that when you speak, do so with a definitive, declarative voice. We don't ask questions in improv because doing so puts all the pressure on your teammates to make a choice and possibly a mistake. Fear of failure has no place on the improv stage, so take a chance!

Asking a question usually signals insecurity on the part of the improviser. Most questions can be loosely translated to "what are we supposed to do?" That's unhelpful to the scene because now not only must your partner make the strong choice you were unwilling to make yourself, but she also must simultaneously pull the questioner back out of his confused limbo. This detracts from the scene in lots of ways, so don't do it.

Another type of question we sometimes see new improvisers ask is the denigrating type—for example, "Why did you do that?" This question also halts the progress of the scene because your scene partner now has to justify her choices rather than furthering the plot. Often, scenes that take this unfortunate turn become scenes about two characters who don't actually like or approve of each other. At best, the question highlights holes in the developing plotline rather than working to plug them. At worst, it derails the action with an attack that calls for a defense, and now we'll never get to the zoo.

Make statements. Be positive. Be bold, uninhibited, and brave.

****** ROI TIP *from* STEVE ******

IMPROVISATIONAL COMEDY HAS trained me to listen and adapt on the fly to what is occurring in the room.

92

In one instance, a prospect reacted to our presentation by saying, "I found your thoughts glib and superficial." Ouch!

Instead of panicking, I improvised on the spot by saying, "Excellent. That's *exactly* what we were hoping you'd say since you have a product that, let's face it, isn't aimed at the next generation of Einsteins. To be blunt, it's glib and superficial, so why not enact a program that meets your target audience exactly where they are?"

That stopped the executive in his tracks. He jingled about ten dollars' worth of coins in his pocket, paced around a bit, and said, "That's positively brilliant. I never thought of connecting with a low IQ target audience by using low IQ tactics. Let's do it!"

They became loyal clients for seven years, but the real value is in the callback. To this day, virtually every time Clayton writes a "thought leadership piece" for us, I let him know immediately that I find it glib and superficial.

Active Listening

In improv, we're always striving for what we call active listening. We learn to observe each other's words and actions in such a way as to actually feel something with each word our scene partner says. The best improvisers listen with the whole body, not just the ears. What does this mean?

Active listening is zeroing in on the words your partner is saying and intentionally tuning into the emotions behind those words.[5] Great actors of all kinds listen to understand rather than listen to respond. It's not about waiting impatiently for your turn to speak. When you listen with your whole body, you are able to sense the exact feeling that your teammate is trying to convey and even feel the same way yourself.

By being so attuned, we enable ourselves to become fully immersed in an improvised moment without any preconceived ideas about what should happen next. When you're truly feeling your partner's expressiveness, you can react honestly not to what you thought she was going to say or what you think she meant. You react empathetically to her feelings, and that enables the entire scene to breathe organically and build in such a way that neither of you knows who's leading because you both are! It's a beautiful thing to behold, and to great improv performers, it's second nature. Their practice, games, and drills build this skill to the point where they're not even consciously thinking about the fact that they're using it anymore. Active listening should always be the goal.

SOME IMPROV GAMES

The tools of improv are the games we play to help us master the key skills of storytelling. In this section, we examine just a few (in reality, there are hundreds) of these games and how we apply them to different business challenges.

First Letter Last Letter

The object of this game is to have a coherent conversation with a beginning, middle, and end that all make sense. Players speak in one complete sentence per player, with the next player obligated to start his first sentence with the last letter the last player used. More accurately, the game should be called "First Sound Last Sound" because English is weird, and this isn't a spelling test. A successful round of this game, might look like this:

BOB: I can't wait to go to the party tonight.
MARIELLE: Totally. I'm going to wear my new shoes!
NYJAH: Zeke is picking up the pizza.
LEE: Understandably, he may be late.
BOB: Take it from me, he'll be there early.
MARIELLE: Even if he has to take the express train.
NYJAH: Never be late for a party when you're the one
    bringing the pizza!

This game teaches a key component of active listening, the skill of waiting until your scene partner is finished speaking before you start. The beauty of it is that it's impossible within the boundaries of the game to begin before you should. After all, who knows what that last letter will be until it's uttered.

So often in business, theater, and life, we are all too eager to jump in and make our own brilliant and salient point before the person who is talking has had enough space to finish her thought. If someone on your team has a nasty habit of interrupting or speaking without building on what was already being said, First Word Last Word will be difficult for that person. Through repeated failure, though, it becomes clear which team members should spend extra time working on active listening and waiting until someone else is finished to speak. This game builds listening skills because you literally can't play without them.

Excuses

The object of this game is to have all players contribute to a project, in this case a narrative that builds on itself. The director starts by asking one player a question in an accusatory tone, such as, "Why are you late?" or "Why didn't you take out the garbage?" That player immediately improvises an excuse. Right away, the next player must build on the excuse and add to it. One variation of this game involves charades, with another group acting out each excuse in turn. Another variation sees our director choosing a winner: the team who gave the best (most plausible, most ridiculous, most original, and so on) excuse as a group. An example of a successful round of Excuses might look like this:

DIRECTOR: Why are you late?
BESSA: The bridge collapsed on my way to work.
ORION: Yes, I think it was caused by the bonfire.
MEGAN: I saw that too. And the river was completely frozen, so no ferry service.
XUAN: Yes, and the president needed the helicopter.
ZIK: I know. He called me to ask for the keys.
EMMI: Definitely. And the trains were delayed due to slime.
AMY: Yes, it was seeping through the walls.
MARLON: Some say it was part of the melting bridge.
BESSA: So I couldn't get here on time!

Excuses is a great game for building a narrative. Collaboration and listening are absolutely essential so that everyone's ideas are duly supported. Teams that need help building and continuing in brainstorms or other content creation sessions often find success warming up as a team with a fun round or two of Excuses.

Cocktail Party

The object of this game is to have multiple storylines connect to one another as part of a larger narrative. Players are divided into groups of two and assigned numbers, pair 1, pair 2, and so on. Paired-up teammates stand close together as though having separate private conversations at a cocktail party. The director shouts out a number and the corresponding pair begins a dialogue during which other pairs pantomime continuing their own conversations. In fact, though, the pantomiming pairs are actively listening to the conversations the unmuted are having. Eventually, the director no longer shouts any numbers, and the scene grows organically.

To achieve the goal, the stories must become interwoven so that the narrative makes sense. A successful round of Cocktail Party might look like this:

DIRECTOR: Pair number three!

THOMAS: I had blueberry pancakes for breakfast today.

JILL: Ooh, my favorite! I just tried that new pancake place on Rosemont Road. So good!

THOMAS: The wife and I have been meaning to go, but her allergies are awful right now.

DIRECTOR: Pair number one!

RAHEEM: I volunteer at the animal shelter right near where you live.

BART: Yeah, the Kitty Kat Kastle! We adopted our cute little Bengal tiger from there.

RAHEEM: I hear those guys can be a bit feisty.

DIRECTOR: Pair number two!

CASSIE: This wine is such a strange color. I've never seen this shade before.

LORETTA: That's because it's made from blueberries, not grapes.

CASSIE: Fermented blueberries! What will they think of next?

DIRECTOR: Open dialogue!

BART: (to Raheem) They're very unusual, but I love unusual creatures.

LORETTA: (to Cassie) A bit unusual maybe, and some people are allergic to blueberries.

JILL: (to Thomas) It's so unusual to develop a blueberry allergy at her age.

RAHEEM: (to Bart) I hear if you feed them blueberries, they calm right down.

CASSIE: (to Loretta) My friend Thomas has unusual taste in wives and pancakes.

THOMAS: (to Jill) Yeah, that's why she had to quit working at the Kitty Kat Kastle!

This sample game would be considered a win because the teams were able to tie their stories together in so many ways. The word *unusual* keeps appearing, as do the themes of blueberries, Bengal tigers, and allergies. Still, the conversations each stand on their own, separate from the conversations the pairs are ostensibly not overhearing.

This game teaches valuable skills such as group thinking, collaboration, listening, and building. It's a more advanced exercise that we use with teams who already have the basics of improvisation under their belts. Teams who excel at Cocktail Party are great storytellers, active listeners who work extremely well together and know how to help others shine. Teams who don't excel at games like this one may learn something from playing them, about how and where their internal communication structures collapse and what they can do to repair them.

IMPROV COMEDY STEP-BY-STEP

By now you're saying, "Can't wait to try some of this stuff. How does it work?" Wait, you mean you weren't saying that at all? Well, could you please say it now, followed by something else bold and positive to accept, build, and continue?

An introductory improv comedy training session, like its stand-up counterpart, usually lasts about three hours. We begin with a lecture, if you will, all about improvisation and what the key skills are. The two of us demonstrate acceptance, building, bold choices, and active listening. We're quite an improv team, the two of us.

After introducing some key skills, we always like to demonstrate the wrong way to do things. One of us will kill a practice scene by saying, "Yes, but . . ." which basically means no. We'll show what happens when someone accepts but doesn't build. We highlight some of the pitfalls that exist for anyone who is just starting to learn improvisational comedy skills.

Next, we divide the group into small improv teams and work with them on a few short-form games, including the ones mentioned in this chapter. With an emphasis on the importance of failure, teamwork, and bold choices, we give each group feedback on the skills demonstrated, with a good mix of praise and constructive criticism.

After a break, we try some long-form scene work and again focus our feedback not on the acting abilities or performance quality of the participants but rather on how well they're applying the key skills. This is because we're not looking to start a new TV show to pitch to HBO; we're looking to improve how we do things back at the office.

At the end, we always like to get a conversation going specifically about how acceptance, building, and teamwork can be used in whatever business sector the group normally inhabits. Sometimes, during this postexercise discussion, key pain points of the overall company will come out, and real conversations about how to address them spontaneously ensue. Once a group is thinking as a team, it's easy to keep them doing so.

A session like this one is typically the second module in an ongoing program of comedy classes that we prescribe with the needs of the individual organization in mind. Building on the stand-up skills acquired in the first session, which help you discover and develop what is funny about yourself, this module teaches you how to create comedic content on the fly as a team. It's a lot of fun, for sure, but the real value comes from learning to apply the lessons of improvisational comedy to make you better at your job.

KEY TAKEAWAYS

- **Acceptance and building**

  Start with yes to get things going.

  Accept others' ideas and build on them.

  Drive the action of the scene with bold choices.

- **Active listening**

    Listen with your whole body.

    Focus not just on your teammates' words but also their feelings.

    Remain open to possibilities you hadn't even thought of yet.

- **Storytelling**

    Establish a clear and vivid setting.

    Drive the action through complication.

    Find a way to end the scene that resolves the complication.

7

SKETCH COMEDY

SKETCH COMEDY CONSISTS of scripted short stories (sometimes called skits or vignettes) performed by a company of actors. While it has its roots in the vaudeville tradition, the form really began to take shape in the early 1950s with Sid Caesar and Imogene Coca's *Your Show of Shows*. By the natural order of things, it evolved into other hilarious TV programs including *The Carol Burnett Show*, *In Living Color*, *Inside Amy Schumer*, and that juggernaut, which will likely never die, *Saturday Night Live*. In the in-person arena, sketch comedy thrives in live performance spaces such as the Groundlings Theatre, the San Francisco Sketch Fest, and the Upright Citizens Brigade Theater.

Sketch comedy often involves social and political commentary, wild and over-the-top recurring characters, and exaggerated impressions of well-known public figures from the towns of Hollywood and Washington. Many sketch comedy performers are also adept at stand-up and improvisation. Great sketches are often written (or at least cowritten) by the performers themselves. Sometimes a sketch idea is lifted directly from a stand-up comic's material. Sometimes it comes from the outcome of an improv game. Regardless of how or why a comic idea is born, if it's scripted and performed as a short scene (either on video or on a stage), that's a sketch.[1]

Great sketch comedians have mastered some important key skills that we think every businessperson should learn, including:

- How to be truthful and compelling in storytelling
- How to get a conversation back on course
- How to display authenticity, empathy, vulnerability, and transparency

KEY SKILLS OF SKETCH COMEDY

As with stand-up and improv, there are key skills required for success in sketch comedy: thesis, observation, and relatability. These skills are learned and developed through the composition and performance of short vignettes. As with all types of comedy writing, the revisions are where the real magic happens. If you really enjoy having a creative toy to tinker around with and keep improving, the world of sketch comedy will quite literally keep you entertained for the rest of your life!

Thesis

The thesis is the point that the sketch is trying to make. The point of Jim Carrey's Fire Marshal Bill is that fire safety education is unnecessarily terror based, or at least it was in Jim's personal experience as an elementary school student in Canada in the 1970s. When a great comedian is confronted with something as bizarre, confusing, and over-the-top as the local volunteer fire department's visit to Jim's third-grade class was, the seed of a great sketch comedy character is born.[2] When a sketch comedy writer has something to say, he says it through his characters.

Observation

In order to arrive at a strong thesis, a comedy creator must first be a keen observer capable of noticing the elements of a person or situation that are not obvious to everyone else. Then, in order to illuminate the point, he uses exaggeration so that these elements are so glaringly obvious as to be hilarious.

We covered Jim Carrey's fire marshal, but Carrey and the rest of the *In Living Color* cast merely paved the way for Comedy Central's *Key and Peele*, whose social commentary was delivered in a perfectly exaggerated package on each excellent episode. One of our favorite sketches from comedy masters Keegan-Michael Key and the aforementioned Jordan Peele is called "Substitute Teacher."[3] In it, we again find ourselves in a classroom, but this time the fish out of water is the substitute teacher, Mr. Garvey, whose background in gritty inner-city classrooms reveals an unusual dynamic in his approach to an assignment in the suburbs.

While never coming off as heavy-handed or even a little bit preachy, Key and Peele present a clear point of view about the differences in inner-city versus suburban schools. The commentary is actually a somber one, that classroom management techniques in different neighborhoods vary far more greatly than perhaps they should, to the detriment of inner-city students' education. Key's portrayal of Mr. Garvey makes us laugh out loud while simultaneously considering and lamenting the status quo. The illumination of this valid social commentary via one fantastic comedy skit is as brilliant as it is sobering.

Observation means seeing things as they are as well as how they should be. The biggest laughs come from the feeling that someone just turned a light switch on in a room where you didn't even know they were off. The best comedy turns reality on its head and causes us to laugh, sure, but more importantly it makes us self-reflect in a way that simple statements of fact or opinion never could. As our favorite Chilean poet-diplomat, the late Pablo Neruda, famously said, "Laughter is the language of the soul."

★ ★ ★ ★ ★ ★ **LOL TIP** *from* **CLAYTON** ★ ★ ★ ★ ★ ★

OBSERVATION IS AT the heart of all comedy, be it stand-up, improv, or sketch. Comedians constantly ask themselves questions like, "What's wrong with this picture?" or "How does this make me feel?" in their ongoing efforts to find a thesis that will strike a chord with audiences. A question like, "What do I wish I could change about this?" can lead to a powerful train of thought that leads to laughter and applause. A big reason people go to comedy clubs or watch sketch comedy on television is an interest in hearing a refreshing take on a topic. From areas as politically charged as capital punishment laws to something as superficial as the latest flavor of Pop-Tart, comedians have strong opinions about everything under the sun, and their audiences are hungry for unique perspectives as well as toaster pastry treats.

> Did you know they have a "frosted chocolate cupcake" flavor now? So good.

Relatability

Every time an audience laughs, the laugh means something. Whether it's, "Wow, I never thought of that before," "Holy cow, I can't believe you just said that," or "The same thing just happened to me last week," hidden within every ha is a statement of what about the performance the audience finds relatable. The more relatable the comic idea, the more connected to the scene the audience feels. The best sketches touch on areas that strike a chord and inspire emotions in addition to laughter.[4]

A classic sketch from *The Kids in the Hall* features Bruce McColloch as the incredibly intense boss of a busy office.[5] The boss character, despite being incredibly over-the-top, is relatable because it's an exaggerated depiction of someone we all know on some level. By sending up an office stereotype, the *Kids* get big laughs at the expense of someone most of us think really deserves it. Take it down a notch, boss man!

FORMS OF SKETCH COMEDY

Parody

Parody means comedy built around the framework of an existing construct or other preexisting material. The audience's familiarity with the target is typically key to making the joke work. *SNL* used the parody form in a clever commercial sketch poking fun at rival network CBS.[6] In the sketch, we see a commercial for a fictional sitcom called *Broken* that panders to Emmy voters in hopes of garnering at least a nomination for Best Comedy. The twist is that the show is not funny at all but touches on the sort of themes that tend to get nominated during award season in all categories. This parody works so well because it lampoons CBS, commercials, and the Emmys all at once! The trite ad format, "Coming this fall to CBS," is so familiar that viewers can instantly latch on to what precisely the joke is and laugh along with the hyperbole that follows.

Song parodies are also very common and relatively easy to create. They work best when everyone already knows the song and the singer very closely follows the original lyrics, changing them just enough to make the song funny. Another secret here is copying the vocal stylings or other trademarks of the original artist in a silly way. The undisputed heavyweight champion of this style for forty years running is Weird Al Yankovic.[7]

Whether you're spoofing a song, a movie trailer, or something else, the parody form relies on the creator's keen powers of observation to notice what is so ridiculous or remarkable about the target. Once that is done, a thesis can be established, and then an exaggeration of the trademark elements of the original can ensue.

Inversion

In the inversion form of sketch comedy, a character is presented doing the opposite of what would normally be expected. Examples include Phil Hartman's Unfrozen Caveman Lawyer,[8] Blake Bennett's Baby Boss,[9] and the unforgettable Damon Wayans as Homie da Clown.[10] The comedy in inversion comes from our surprise in seeing an expected character do the unexpected. It's pretty easy to dream up your own inversion. How about a depressed cheerleader, a tobacco-spitting redneck with a PhD in nuclear physics, or a yoga instructor with a terrible temper? All of these characters have potential for hilarity.

Exaggeration

Exaggeration is taking the familiar and distorting it, particularly at its extremes. Examples include Dave Chappelle's over-the-top portrayal of Rick James[11] to pretty much everything they ever did on *Portlandia*.[12] Once observation has occurred, a thesis can come through in a clearer and more relatable way through the effective use of exaggeration. By exaggerating what's funny, unfair, boring, hypocritical, backward, silly, unusual, clever, or wrong about our subject, we shed light on these qualities through the exaggerated sketch.

TOOLS OF SKETCH COMEDY

Brainstorming

When you first set out to write a comedy sketch, you need to brainstorm to answer questions like the Five Ws (who, what, when, where, and why) but also to figure out the desired length and tone of your piece. We like to start with our thesis. What are we trying to say? And then, we figure out how to say it. The brainstorming process is a success if it helps you come up with ideas for a setting, plot, or a character or two. These can all be very rough ideas to be fleshed out later, or in some cases they're more vivid. A few important things to remember in brainstorming are:

- Accept all the creative and wild ideas.
- Build on other participants' ideas.
- Don't criticize other collaborators' ideas.
- Aim for quantity over quality.
- Make the brainstorming session visual.

Improvisation

Once we have a thesis, a character, a setting, and maybe a few other elements loosely in place, we continue the brainstorm on our feet in the form of an improvisation. We're basically going to practice long-form improv here with the goal of discovering the key elements of our eventual script: premise, complication, escalation, and payoff. We'll discuss these elements next, but for now keep in mind that the skills of improv explored in the previous chapter—acceptance, building, and teamwork—apply here.

Premise

The premise is the comic idea behind the sketch. It should be clear what time and place we're in and what's happening in the first five or ten seconds. Two cheerleaders practice during non-school hours,[13] an inner-city version of *Mister Rogers' Neighborhood*,[14] a woman shops in an upscale clothing store.[15] The audience must be able to identify the premise of a sketch almost immediately.

Complication

In all types of fictional narrative, some sort of obstacle must present itself. This obstacle, the complication of the story, is the driving force behind the action of the scene. The cheerleaders are actually awful at cheerleading. Mr. Rogers has a neighbor who threatens to call the police and end the TV show. Our shopper realizes the store is only for very thin women and can't find anything in her size. Through complication, we show the audience what problem we want to address in the sketch through our characters and their reactions to the obstacle.

Obstacles are necessary to drive a scene, but they needn't come in the form of a villain or an outside force. Often in comedy, the character has a flaw that is the obstacle she tries to overcome to comic effect. On *Portlandia*, recurring characters Toni and Candace take themselves too seriously to take a joke, have healthy relationships, or even sell one single book, ever.[16] The comedy comes from the relatability of the characters and how much trouble they have overcoming their obstacle of just being too serious for their own good.

Sketch comedy is wide open in terms of genre, setting, plots, characters, and styles.

KEY TAKEAWAYS

- **Strong point of view**

  Find a clear opinion and a way to express it.

  Ensure that your message resonates with your audience.

  Create unexpected or ironic ways to share.

- **Exaggeration**

  Use broad characters and plot to drive points home.

  Take familiar elements and expand or distort them.

Have a tongue-in-cheek tone and trust them to get it.

- **Storytelling**

   Play with surprising settings and premises.

   Make the day a significant one in the character's life.

   Get to the complication early; the laughs come from the struggle.

PART THREE

THE

DIY

OF

LOL

HOW TO USE COMEDY SKILLS *in* BUSINESS

8

STAND-UP COMEDY IN BUSINESS

BACK IN CHAPTER 5, we looked at how comedians develop material and performances to provide great, memorable experiences for the audiences. In this section, we're going to focus on how you as a business leader can leverage the skills of stand-up to expand the depth and breadth of the conversations critical to engaging with your stakeholder audiences. Comedians have charisma, and let's be honest, most of your job descriptions don't include that word. But they absolutely should, considering the many diverse audiences with whom you and your brand must engage.

Charismatic individuals, regardless of whether they're in the public, private, or nonprofit sectors, have the innate ability to attract attention and deepen relationships. By understanding the magnetism that goes along with charisma, you and your organization can break through the sea of sameness and outflank your competition. Research shows that the average human being's attention span is 8.25 seconds, shorter than that of a fish.[1] In order to keep all eyes on you, therefore, you've got to be compelling and charismatic in less time than that. After all, there are plenty of fish in the sea, and the clock is ticking.

Charisma is, of course, not limited to entertainers. Quite a few politicians, business leaders, and others exude charisma. We'd include such notables as John F. Kennedy, Ronald Reagan, Steve Jobs, Daymond John, and Jim Cramer in our list of most charismatic nonperformers.

JFK, for example, was noted for using witticisms to deflect negative or irrelevant questions in his many White House press conferences.[2] And when Jobs was at the helm of Apple, the company never even held a single press event. Instead, Jobs would take the stage when the time was right and absolutely dazzle those in attendance (as well as millions watching a live stream) as he unveiled the company's latest product.[3] Sadly, the same approach didn't work out quite as well for Jobs wannabe Elizabeth Holmes.[4]

Whether it was Kennedy explaining why he was penalizing the steel companies for an outrageous price hike or John explaining how he became an entrepreneur selling hats on the street corner, we simply couldn't take our eyes off either. And that, dear reader, is the closest we can come to defining charisma. Believe us when we say: mastering the art of stand-up comedy, or even just trying it a few times, can help you enhance *your* personal charisma, whatever the hell that is.

APPLYING KEY STAND-UP COMEDY SKILLS TO BUSINESS

Great stand-up comedians know how to connect with vastly diverse audiences. As we explored in chapter 5, they do so by embracing vulnerability, emotional fullness, and sensitivity. In this section, we'll look at these skills again, but this time from a business standpoint.

Vulnerability

Vulnerability in business means admitting one is not omniscient. There's always room for improvement, after all. Admitting that one doesn't have all the answers or has made a mistake, once thought a deadly error in the business world, is now expected. Ignore vulnerability in today's corporate climate at your own risk.

One need only look back a few years to the cringeworthy efforts of chief executive officers from Big Tobacco, the Big Three automakers, Big Pharma, and of course Wells Fargo to see how poorly the old-school, autocratic "It's good to be the king" mentality no longer wins in court or, critically, *in the court of public opinion.*

In almost every instance where CEOs, their legal beagles, in-house PR shills, and other posse members sit across a video- and still-camera–filled chasm that separates them from righteously angered and shocked Senate or House representatives, they either provide one-word answers, roll their eyes, say they have no knowledge of any wrongdoing, plead the Fifth, or all of the above.

Many of today's CEOs *know* the importance of vulnerability, especially in the immediate aftermath of a mega crisis. Stonewalling is no longer accepted and will, in fact, backfire. Every single constituent, from a local farmer whose pig mysteriously went belly-up after sipping contaminated water to an institutional investor who stands to lose billions as a result of his investing in the wrong company at the wrong time (think Silicon Valley Bank), expects an admission of fault, an apology, a willingness to fix whatever happened, an assurance it will never happen again, and a closure that will either see the offending executive suffer a severe financial penalty and/or don an orange jumpsuit and relocate to a Sing Sing cell alongside Johnny One Tooth and He Loathe Me. (Note: He Loathe Me does *not* suffer fools or cellmates gladly but Johnny One Tooth *will* mix up a mean bowl of pasta if he takes a liking to you.)

Doing the right thing, being vulnerable and admitting when you haven't, is a risk you must take to attract and retain the best and brightest in today's corporate jungle. We've seen a few examples of CEOs actually admitting fault and accepting blame at the same time they're announcing downsizings. One is Stripe CEO Patrick Collison, who shouldered full responsibility for having overexpanded during the 2020 pandemic. In a heartfelt email to all employees being laid off, Collison shared, "There's no good way to do a layoff, but we're going to do our best to treat everyone leaving as respectfully as possible and to do whatever we can to help." And he backed that up with a virtually unprecedented package of support services that included a minimum of fourteen weeks of severance pay, six months of health care, and career support that included a first-of-its-kind alumni network for those affected by the changes.[5] It takes a vulnerable and authentic CEO to shoulder the blame for misreading market conditions, admitting that he expanded too quickly and didn't anticipate the unexpected.

Embracing vulnerability while simultaneously holding herself accountable may leave a CEO open to criticism, but it also engenders loyalty, admiration, and, most important, trust from every key stakeholder. Citigroup CEO Jane Fraser told *Fortune CEO Daily* in November 2022, "I view empathy as a hard skill. It's not soft. This isn't about being nice. This gives you a competitive edge. Empathy in our workforce has enabled us to attract and retain an extraordinary group of people in our organization. We have become an employer of choice. People want to work here because of the positions we've taken."

Beyond the recent seismic downturns in sectors across the board, we've all witnessed and experienced the Great Resignation, Bare Minimum Mondays, Quiet Quitting, and its evil (or good) cousin, Fast Firing. While there's no surefire way to retain employees who simply want to do something completely different, a comedy-based culture can certainly help mitigate the damage.

At Peppercomm, we're currently working with a number of *Fortune* 500 corporations that have experienced turnover rates in excess of 40 percent. In each instance, our number one goal is to demonstrate how committed each organization is to the personal and professional health and well-being of every employee. And, trust us, bringing employees together who remain separated by a remote work culture can put the brakes on mass resignation.

Emotional Fullness

As we explored in chapter 5, the best performers are eager and willing to share their true feelings with their audiences. This can be a daunting thought for many leaders who are accustomed to keeping things close to the vest. Sharing emotion is not a sign of weakness but rather strength. Of course, it must be done in the appropriate way and with the sensibilities of one's corporate culture front of mind. You can't share all things with all people, but finding moments to let your emotions breathe can be liberating for you and your stakeholders.

✱ ✱ ✱ ✱ ✱ ROI TIP *from* STEVE ✱ ✱ ✱ ✱ ✱

I PLUMBED THE depths of my emotional fullness to deliver spontaneous remarks to my employee base on the day we announced our acquisition by Ruder Finn, one of the world's largest public relations firms.

I was joined in our Manhattan conference room by Kathy Bloomgarden, the most excellent chief executive officer of RF.[6] After Kathy spoke about how important Peppercomm was to her firm's existing and future planning, she turned it over to me.

I quickly enumerated the myriad business benefits of being acquired *and* being allowed to remain a separate brand with a separate P&L and remaining in our existing building. I then spoke about what the liquidity event (as we stock analyst types are wont to say) meant to me personally.

I told my employees that I'd always considered Peppercomm to be my third child (after Chris and Catharine, respectively). And just as I had carefully and gently nurtured, encouraged, embraced, chastised, and adjusted my love for my children, I did the same with Peppercomm. I shared with the Peppercommers what I'd been telling every employee since our founding in 1995: "Peppercomm will always be Peppercomm's most important client." I stressed how important it was for me to do the right thing for myself, the right thing for my employees, and the right thing for Peppercomm.

I said I felt the RF acquisition had achieved all of those objectives. And, as I closed my brief remarks, I ended by

---

saying, "The two most important moments in my life were watching Chris and Catharine being born. Knowing that I've done the right thing for my third child, I can look each of you in the eye and say that selling Peppercomm now ranks as 2A on my Top Ten list."

I teared up, as did many of the Peppercommers standing a few feet away from me (or it could have just been the reaction to the semitoxic emissions from our heating system), when I ended by saying, "I am so happy for each and every one of you."

And that heartfelt, emotional fullness created the exact response I'd hoped for. While there were the usual questions about benefits and the reporting structure, all my employees knew I was thinking of them and ensuring that everything they loved would stay the same and a whole new world of opportunities would be awaiting them, courtesy of Ruder Finn. And that's exactly how things have worked out since the acquisition.

In Collison's aforementioned email to the laid-off employees, he expressed his feelings fully and openly. The phrases "I'm sorry," "taken pride," "it pains us," "we care," "we appreciate," "regret two very consequential mistakes," and "today is a sad day" all appear in the heartfelt note filled with the language of emotions. The fact that it was accompanied by the unprecedented severance package served to punctuate the fact that Collison meant every word he wrote that day.

Unfortunately, many business leaders still equate vulner-ability with weakness. The fact remains there are countless Elon Musk and Jamie Dimon types out there who think emotional fullness is best expressed by an impersonal email terminating fifteen thousand employees right before Thanksgiving.[7] Or like David Solomon, CEO of Goldman Sachs (which recorded record revenues of $59.3 billion in 2021), deciding that his employees should no longer be given free coffee at the office.[8] They need to shell out four dollars for their café latte. Now that's what we call empathy and putting people ahead of profits. *Not!*

On the other hand, a great example of a CEO who is open and self-deprecating is Reed Hastings of Netflix, the Yin to Musk's Yang. "I take pride in making as few decisions as possible, as opposed to making as many as possible."[9] Hastings trusts his employees and empowers them to take risks, provided they're willing to own their mistakes and learn from them. Which CEO would you rather report to?

When to Say When

Just like stand-up comedians, businesspeople need to "be in the room" to determine exactly when to turn their emo-tional fullness on, off, or shift into neutral. Determining exactly how and when to put the pedal to the metal on your feelings in a business meeting is a *very* tricky proposition for the uninitiated. You first need to bring your authentic self to any meeting.

* * * * * * ROI TIP *from* STEVE * * * * * *

I HAD THE misfortune of witnessing a top executive going a bridge too far in sharing his feelings with a reporter from *Crain's Chicago Business*. We had media trained the executive, and the goal was to properly position his company as a new competitor to local banks in the Windy City. He nailed every single message point but failed to put the brakes on his enthusiasm. As we were walking to the elevator, the reporter said, "Gosh, I love your office space." Our exuberant client volunteered, "Oh, well we've just taken a lease on thirty-five thousand square feet on Michigan Avenue." As a result of this lapse in judgment, instead of getting the headline we wanted, *CCB* ran with the headline from hell: "XYZ Announces Relocation Plan." They did relocate and the executive was fired before he could pack his bag for the move. He lost his cool, let his guard down, and blew our one shot to make a big splash in the market.

Whenever we first introduce our stand-up comedy training program to a new company, we first insist on buy-in from the very top. After a brief lecture on the theories of comedy and some demonstrations of a few key skills, we ask the CEO, CHRO, CMO, or CCO to take the stage. This disarms the other employees in the room because it shows that the boss is invested, is in on the joke. The leaders recognize the importance of learning these skills and are willing to get their hands a little dirty to show everyone in the room that they take their work very seriously, but perhaps don't take themselves too seriously.

Often, a top executive's performance is dynamic and inspiring. Many times it isn't. In the end, the fact that this person just attempted to learn a new skill right before our very eyes, and risked abject failure and life-altering humiliation in the process, is the win. By taking this risk, the leader demonstrates empathy (and, obviously, the all-important aforementioned tenet of stand-up, vulnerability) and removes any perceived barriers others might assume exist. (For example, *Is it cool to walk into the boss's office with an idea?*)

In one recent training session, the newly minted CEO of a multibillion-dollar international powerhouse stood in front of his direct reports and told them about his life growing up as the son of a vicar in jolly old England. In the midst of puberty, the tale went, his voice was changing, and parishioners routinely mistook him for his father. In one unfortunate case, a parishioner asked him to deliver the service for the burial of a recently departed loved one. His direct reports laughed out loud at the comedy of errors. Hearing the story really humanized this leader to his entire staff, many of whom were actually meeting him in person for the very first time.

Emilia Bunea, PhD, witnessed a leader taking a chance on a high-risk joke when she worked as CFO of a health care company. In her article "Can Humor Make You a Better Leader?" Bunea writes:

In a progress meeting on building a new hospital wing, the project manager brought dire news: the passageway between the new and the old wing was one inch too low, and ambulances could not go through. I started running numbers in my mind; this would mean serious rework and budget overruns.

There was a moment of silence while everyone was busy panicking, until the operations director mused: "Have you tried Vaseline?" The roar of laughter that followed defused the tension and allowed the team to start brainstorming on creative ways to solve the problem instead of competing on who best deflects the blame.[10] That joke became legendary in the company. But had the CEO, who was also present, frowned instead of joining in the Vaseline-induced laughter, the Ops director's rise to the top would have needed a great deal more lubricant.[11]

In the end, you have to be yourself. If you've traditionally been seen as an introvert by your peers, you cannot suddenly become Michael Che at the next weekly Zoom check-in call. Instead, you really need to embrace the tenets of stand-up comedy as described in these chapters and figure out exactly what level of authentic emotional fullness is appropriate to you. How much of your unique sense of humor should you bring to each meeting?

Diandra Binney, US head of communications at Xero, likes to share a little of her own funny side at work:

As with many jobs, there are certain actions that repeat themselves week after week. Comedy training provides the green light to make those moments lighter, memorable, and more meaningful. After getting to know a new internal client, I try to start every call with either a funny anecdote about something that's happening in pop culture, a current event, or my own life (which has its fair share of absurdity). I find this approach serves to disarm my colleagues and start us off with a laugh before getting into more serious matters. It makes everyone smile and feel more at ease, and encourages everyone to be lighthearted during what might otherwise be just another status call. It also deepens relationships in the long run.

Keep in mind, dear reader, that Diandra had been trained in comedy for many years before ever injecting it into conversations with her coworkers. This takes time. Rome wasn't built in a day. And some would say Penn Station should never have been built at all.

Sensitivity

We have explored how comedy performances are tailored, to some degree, to specific audiences. From doing stand-up, Steve has developed the sensitivity required to take the temperature in business settings great and small as well, and adjust accordingly.

* * * * * * ROI TIP *from* STEVE * * * * * *

WE'RE OFTEN INVITED to participate in what's known in our industry as "cattle calls." We know going into these presentations that we're up against four or five top competitors and will have about ninety minutes to seal the deal.

Before beginning our presentation, I always try to read the room by gauging the vibes of the client-side attendees. Instead of asking them about sports or the weather, I'll test their openness to laughter. I do so by addressing the very real possibility that something will go wrong with our PowerPoint technology. "Please raise your hands and let me know if part of your selection process will be based on our technology prowess. If so, we might as well leave now because I guarantee one of the videos or charts we'd like to show you won't work."

That sort of unexpected statement elicits one of two responses that enables me to anticipate the tone of the meeting: blank stares or laughter from someone on the client side. In the former case, I know we're sailing into a category-five hurricane. But when I hear that first chuckle, I know I've struck a chord and invariably the person who laughed will share her own horror story about a tech SNAFU.

In other instances, we've entered a prospective client's conference room only to find copies of the leave behinds from other agencies who had gone before us scattered across the table. That's a *very* bad sign since it sends an immediate signal that the prospect doesn't respect the time and effort that went into each firm's presentation.

So, on the occasions where that's occurred, I'll ask the senior decision maker, "Do you mind if we flip through the presentations made by our competitors to make sure we don't suggest some of the same ideas?"

Again, that will elicit one of two responses: Either (a) the chief communications officer will laugh and ask someone to clear the table, or (b) respond with a shrug of the shoulders and say, "Do as you please." The latter response usually leads me to end the meeting right then and there because we want to enjoy the client teams with whom we partner (and avoid a-holes at all costs).

In 2020, Peppercomm had to repitch the MINI USA account to retain them as a client. We went back to MINI's breakthrough "Not Normal" campaign to challenge our account team in our brainstorming process. We developed ideas through the lens of being "not normal" and asked the team to share ideas around a storyline of what would be not normal for this car brand.

We built stories as a team, one word at a time. The goal was to arrive at ideas that connected with prospective customers who saw themselves as outside the norm. The team storytelling brought us to a theme of Unconditional Love and initiatives including: an adoption and reunion event for all dogs named Cooper; a hunt for D. B. Cooper[12]; and a Where to Get Off campaign making MINI the *Michelin Guide* to roadside fine dining no matter where you are in America.

Due in part to our sensitivity and having our fingers on the pulse of the client and their customers, Peppercomm was re-signed as MINI's agency of record, a position we still enjoy as of this writing (fingers crossed and axles greased).

Crossing the Line

Earlier, we talked about our favorite slogan, "When in doubt, leave it out." Still, within businesses, there is often an understandable reticence to introduce stand-up training for fear that it may cross the boundaries of diversity, equity, and inclusiveness. Obviously, nobody wants the comedy training to do permanent damage in these incredibly sensitive times, and we're not advocating for that either. In fact, our academic cohort, Malcolm Frierson, addresses this very real concern at length in the afterword to this remarkably sensitive and carefully constructed book, which we hope will never offend any person, place, or thing, now or at any point in the past or future.

Rob Duda, Peppercomm's automotive and transportation strategist and gearhead par excellence, picked the wrong time and place with the wrong prospect and learned a valuable lesson about listening first and taking the temperature before going for laughs:

> We had a highly anticipated new business pitch with the entire corporate communications team for a global tire manufacturer. We thought it was a no-brainer to open the presentation with some stand-up comedy material. They seemed friendly and laid back in our initial discussions, so I gladly volunteered to regale them with some jokes of my own, since I was going to be their main day-to-day account lead if we won the business. What better way to break the ice, especially since I had just used this material onstage and had absolutely killed? Unfortunately, in this instance, the

only death was our chances of winning these tire guys as a client.

I confidently launched into what I thought was a surefire routine revolving around my love for meteorology. Barometric pressure, cloud cover, warm fronts, all great punch lines, right? Crickets.

When I finished my "set," we moved on to our PowerPoint presentation, but clearly I had already sucked the air out of the room, and it wasn't coming back. When we reached the end of our presentation, the prospect thanked us for our time and energy but informed us that theirs was a "humorless" culture, and we simply wouldn't fit in.

We were as deflated as four flat tires. But it's always darkest before the dawn, and believe it or not, we were contacted within a month by their direct competitor, who hired us and remains one of our major clients even to this day.

As we mentioned, an essential component of any creative endeavor is failure. Today's employees want the workplace to be a safe space wherein they are not only allowed to fail but encouraged to learn through experimentation and share the lessons learned (good, bad, and ugly) with peers. A study published in the *Journal of Managerial Psychology* found that the use of "employee humor" about undesired results can lead to "workgroup cohesion, health, and coping effectiveness, as well as decreased burnout, stress, and work withdrawal."[13] In other words, learn to laugh it off, because failure is an extremely important part of the process.

★ ★ ★ ★ ★ ★ ROI TIP *from* STEVE ★ ★ ★ ★ ★ ★

MY EMPLOYEES ROUTINELY see me fail or not elicit any laughter when I perform onstage. I embrace that apparent setback since it shows that I'm very comfortable with failing (as long as I've learned a lesson from bombing). And, invariably, I do learn one or two new things I know to never repeat. I firmly believe that learning from one's failures is a key attribute common among all successful people. In fact, many legendary figures past and present failed again and again until they finally got it right. Thomas Edison famously said, "I haven't failed. I've just found ten thousand ways that won't work." Other notable failures:

- Michael Jordan was cut from his high school varsity basketball team in 1978.
- The Wright brothers failed for two years to build a plane that would stay aloft before finally breaking through in 1903.
- Marie Curie's fingers were literally burned and scarred from working with radium on her way to winning the Nobel Prize for Chemistry in 1911.
- Jay-Z's music was turned down by every major record label in the US before he cofounded a label, Roc-a-Fella Records, in 1995.
- Aubrey Plaza was rejected by *Saturday Night Live* in 2003 but guest hosted in 2023.
- Stephen King pinned all of his rejection letters to his wall.

I believe that my own openness about my failures and weaknesses has served as a true catalyst in our internal communications at Peppercomm. Thanks to the training and my always sending around emails with ideas that are routinely rejected by account team members, I love to not only poke fun at myself but encourage all our employees to follow suit.

Just like comedians know how to handle bombing, executives need to have the ability to redirect a meeting that's obviously going south. Case in point: If our *big* idea is met by deafening silence, I will often stand up, walk around the conference room table, and say, "I know you adored our *big* idea. In fact, I can see the wheels inside your heads spinning right now. You're thinking to yourselves: 'What an amazing concept! I know exactly how we can implement it.'"

If that doesn't elicit at least a smile or two, I'll know we're toast and signal my team to wrap up the presentation right then and there.

In other instances, though, I've "saved" the near-death experience and converted it into a beautiful long-term relationship.

And I'm not the only one. Years ago, my colleague Ann Barlow, Peppercomm's West Coast president and senior partner, had been endeavoring to get an introduction to Panasonic. She says:

> We had strong consumer electronics experience, and it was clear to me that Panasonic was looking to up their game, maybe with a new agency. One late afternoon,

I called one of my executive contacts at Panasonic for the thirty-seventh time in an attempt to set up a meeting. It happened to be Halloween, and his assistant had left early to take her kids trick-or-treating, so I finally got through to him. He listened to our credentials and ideas, and agreed to meet. I was thrilled to finally have the door open, or at least cracked, and I gathered all my colleagues to help get everything ready for the big pitch.

Our team prepared for several weeks, conducting research, developing insights and ideas, and coming up with what we thought was a very solid plan. When the big day arrived, six of us entered a large boardroom to meet with their team. They sat along one side of an aircraft carrier–sized table, and we took our seats on the other. To say the setup was intimidating would be like saying Kanye West is opinionated. With a deep breath, I kicked off the presentation by thanking the Panasonic executives for their time. I then leaned forward to gesture to the slide being projected and almost instantly my chair slid out from under me!

In a terror-induced feat of speed and dexterity, I somehow grabbed onto the giant conference table and held on for dear life, managing to remain upright as my chair skidded back several feet. I stood up, took hold of the chair, steered it back in front of the table, and took my seat. With a deadpan expression, I explained that we at Peppercomm believe icebreakers are an important way to start a meeting.

We won the business.

Still another member of our executive team, Melissa Vigue, knew how to keep her sense of humor in the face of an embarrassing fall:

I'm standing in one of those football field–sized conference rooms at a major restaurant holding company preparing to facilitate a brainstorm for some thirty-five-plus senior executives. It was my first interaction with these casual food superpowers, and I'd forgotten to pack my contact lenses and wasn't used to wearing my glasses at that point.

Confidently sauntering toward a large group of the most important people in the room, the clients I desperately wanted to impress, I failed to notice one of those super handy "brainstorm starters" we like to use in these situations, a.k.a. a Tonka toy truck. I stepped right on the toy, rolled my ankle along with the truck and a whirligig office chair in my path of destruction, and let out an alarmed squeal on my way down to the carpet. I crashed spectacularly into a glass wall, which thankfully didn't break but absolutely reverberated from the strain of the collision, only partially covering the sound of the string of expletives escaping my mouth. My glasses went flying off my face and hit the CCO right on the forehead. A collective gasp filled the room followed by ten seconds of absolute silence, accentuating the fact that all eyes were squarely on me.

I jumped up spryly and announced, "Now that I have your attention, let's get started!" The relief and laughter that followed broke the ice immediately, followed by a round of applause. I like to think I added some pizzazz to what otherwise could have been an extremely dull meeting. You're welcome.

FORMS OF STAND-UP COMEDY

Observational

Earlier, we emphasized the importance of emotional fullness in observational stand-up comedy. At Peppercomm, we saw the emotion of comfort in action at one of our weekly in-person staff meetings. Steve happened to glance over to a far corner of the conference room and asked the young account supervisor who had sardined herself into the nook why she didn't want to sit in one of the chairs closer to the screen showing twenty-five of our remote workers. She responded by saying, "I really like this corner a lot." Steve replied, "Understood. And duly noted. Team: from now on, the southeast section of this conference room will be forever known as 'Keri's Corner.'" Since then, no one has sat in that corner, even when Keri is traveling or out sick. We even have a little sign designating it as Keri's Corner. It's an inside joke that we all love, and it keeps a smile on everyone's face, especially Keri.[14]

It may not seem like much, but using observational humor in the workplace not only can be incredibly funny and binding, but it can establish new shared experiences that are inside jokes known only by you and your colleagues. In our opinion, that's more binding than Elmer's Glue. (Ever wonder who Elmer was or if he ever inhaled his own product?)

Anecdotal

We've learned that anecdotal stand-up is typically based in underdog stories. A great place to start is "What's your most embarrassing story?" Audiences love to hear about our, shall we say, humbling experiences. Our friend and Accenture chief communications officer Stacey Jones has never performed stand-up comedy, but if she did, she might draw from a meta experience she once had in an alternate universe:

> We all know that learning to use new technologies is a must, but it can also be daunting and extremely humbling. About a year ago, I was interviewed about, and in, the metaverse just as I was learning to navigate it, and we had a whole filming plan in place. Everyone was nervous about how it might go, including the film crew, the organizers, all of us.
>
> The interviewer and I ventured onto a basketball court in the metaverse, where I started to feel pretty confident. After all, back in the day, I was quite the basketball star. But that was real life; in the metaverse, I could barely find the basket! It was like I was throwing bricks, and I missed every shot spectacularly, not even close. I started laughing at the silliness of the situation. Soon the entire crew joined in because, trust me, see-

ing me try to sink those meta baskets was . . . funny. I think all the laughter put the team running the filming at ease, though, and ended up setting a great "human" tone to the whole filming experience.[15]

Our own executive vice president and chief client officer, Maggie O'Neill, is the Peppercomm version of a star who was fearless enough to share an uncomfortable truth in a major new business pitch:

I had just had my appendix removed two days before the new business pitch. While I probably should not have traveled, I did; but that's a work-life balance story for another day. Kicking off the meeting, I raised the issue of my fragile health right away, to put everyone at ease. I also let everyone in the room know that:

- I may need to stand during the meeting because of the pain, so please don't freak out.
- Our team had a secret word to use if I needed to exit (Pellegrino).
- I would likely not die (my doctor's words, not mine).

Letting the prospect in on the joke, if you will, not only set up a more relaxed atmosphere, but it also revealed an authentic, personal story that helped us connect in a very human way with everyone on the other side of the table. We only said Pellegrino once and won the business. They became our largest client.

Using anecdotal comedy, sharing funny and authentic stories in an amusing and vulnerable way, differentiates you and your brand. It can also ease tensions and remove barriers that might exist between you and successfully closing a deal, getting a budget approved, or just helping others to smile and relax. It can even help you get a free bottle of Pellegrino or Pepto-Bismol, depending on how much trouble your GI tract is giving you, post-appendectomy.

Put-Down

We've discussed how put-down humor is delicate and requires buy-in from not only the audience but also the target. On social media, put-down comedy reigns supreme. We happen to be big fans of companies that embrace this particular technique in their external storytelling, keeping the tone light and fun while building a strong social media presence through well-constructed and well-placed zingers. Our favorite example is Wendy's, the undisputed first lady of fast food. The shtick, if you will, is that Wendy is sassy, irreverent, and unapologetic when replying to other social media accounts, especially those representing competing fast-food chains.[16] The results are hilarious but also measurable versus direct competitors. Wendy's Twitter following is 3.9 million compared with 1.6 million and 850,000 for KFC and Arby's, respectively. Put-down humor can be a great form of revenge, a dish best served hot with a side of fries.

Companies regularly ask us to help them come up with some "roast" material to be performed at the retirement dinner for a high-level executive. The first question we ask is always, "Does she know she's going to be roasted?" If you've ever seen this sort of performance on TV, it may look like the person being eviscerated isn't expecting the awful things that her friends are saying about her. But the whole point of a roast is to punch up at someone who can definitely take a joke! As Chris Rock learned at the 2022 Academy Awards, if the target of your joke isn't expecting the punch line, the comic himself can receive an actual punch in the face!

✶ ✶ ✶ ✶ ✶ ✶ ROI TIP *from* STEVE ✶ ✶ ✶ ✶ ✶ ✶

WE LOVE PUT-DOWN humor at Peppercomm, but even we can miss the mark at times, and I'm guessing that's not unique to our organization. It's a tricky thing to pull off, and I'm the first to admit when it's time to take one in the L column.

One night after a company happy hour, we all shared stories about one senior executive I will call Hank, who always seemed to lose or forget something. Sometimes it was his briefcase, other times his laptop. And, on one memorable occasion, he even forgot to bring his luggage back home from an overnight trip to Washington, DC. Who does that?

Regardless, whenever Hank finally realized he'd made a big mistake he would cry out, "Oh fudge!"

So I had the not-very-bright idea of collecting all the "Oh fudge!" stories (and there must have been at least twenty-five), having them professionally bound in a hand-some leather booklet and enlisting Doshia, a very willing middle manager (who had contributed two stories of her own), to preempt our summer party with a special event.

I grabbed the microphone, got everyone's attention, and asked Doshia and Hank to join me at the podium for

THE ROI OF LOL

> a presentation. I handed the microphone over to Doshia, and she began reading the first story. By the time she got halfway through the second tale, I realized I'd made an egregious mistake. I hadn't alerted Hank that we'd be sharing some of his more memorable mishaps. If looks could kill, the book you're reading today would have a single author instead of two. I quickly pulled the plug (literally) and asked the band to strike up a suitable tune. I think they played "Taps."

If that weren't bad enough, Steve really learned his lesson regarding the misuse of put-down humor in an internal management committee meeting in our New York office.

✶ ✶ ✶ ✶ ✶ ✶ ROI TIP *from* STEVE ✶ ✶ ✶ ✶ ✶ ✶

WE HAD JUST won a major assignment from one of the Big Three automakers. Our job was to heighten awareness of the client's trucks in the great state of Texas. One of my partners was so eager to share the news that she blurted out, "Hey, everyone, we just won 'Trucks for Texas!'" One of our other executives asked, "How big is Texas?" He was wondering how large the budget for Trucks for Texas would be. I replied, "If memory serves, Texas is the third-largest state in the nation."

Laughter filled the room at my sarcastic quip, but none from my colleague to whom it had been served. He was equal parts humiliated and furious, his face redder than the Lone Star State in an election year. Realizing I had failed to clue him in ahead of time as to the size and scope of the assignment, I pulled him aside to apologize. He wasn't having it and suggested I stick a cattle prod deep in the heart of Texas.

I never meant to embarrass one of my peers in front of all his direct reports, but that's exactly what happened in the conference room that morning. As a mea culpa, from that day forward, I was extra careful to not even mention the Dallas Cowboys, Lance Armstrong, or barbecued brisket in his presence ever again.

STAND-UP COMEDY TECHNIQUES

Setups and Punch Lines

We have examined how clear setups and surprising, vivid punch lines are keys to performing stand-up, but they're also fundamental to breaking through the information overload that constantly bombards and distracts us.

The best brands understand how to use the power of the unexpected to craft campaigns that are shared and, critically, remembered. "Most brands do the expected and, as a result, bore their audiences. The most successful campaigns engage the audience in a new or unexpected way with a certain intelligence, a certain creativity, and a certain juxtaposition that elicits the response 'Oh, I never expected that,'" said Rupen Desai. "Think of breakthrough campaigns that used slogans, tunes, or aphorisms that eventually became part of the lexicon, beginning with Alka-Seltzer's 'Plop,

Plop, Fizz, Fizz,' to Wendy's 'Where's the Beef?' to Bud Light's 'Whasssssup?' chant." These campaigns have all far outlived their life expectancy, in part because of the unexpected nature of their punch lines.

"The ALS Ice Bucket Challenge[17] is a great example of a truly bizarre idea that circled the world many times over and became the gold standard for countless other campaigns aimed at raising money for social causes," Desai added.

Several years ago, Peppercomm was tapped by financial services firm Genworth to create a communications program designed to educate Americans on how they can save more money. The challenges we faced were twofold: First, the conversation around saving money was old and cluttered with many brands offering solutions for how to save more. Second, research showed that most Americans simply weren't in the habit of saving money. How could we help to change that?

Delving into the research, we learned that 71 percent of Americans felt they "did not have enough money to contribute to savings." In reality, many were spending large amounts on nonessentials such as fine dining, flashy jewelry, and expensive coffee. Leveraging this insight, we decided to flip the savings conversation on its head with a lighthearted program that served to both educate and inspire.

The campaign we created was called National $tart Out $avings Day. We developed a list of ten things Americans could do to save more money. To bring this concept to life, we first calculated what luxuries people were spending their hard-earned cash on and discovered a sizable portion of disposable income was going toward expensive coffee. There were other categories, of course, but this one really caught our attention and gave us the same boost as a triple espresso! We knew we were onto something rich, aromatic, and newsworthy, so we got to work.

We designed a cardboard mailer in the form of a coffee cup in a box, which contained a packet of instant freeze-dried coffee from arabica beans. We mailed our paper coffee cups to members of the media. The enclosed letter read: "Is this cup worth $30,000? It could be."

The morning of our launch, local news anchors across the country held up their coffee cups to the cameras, asking the viewing audience, "Could this cup be worth $30,000? Find out after these messages." The campaign was an overwhelming success and created millions of media impressions in the markets most important to Genworth's future success. Talk about a buzz!

Act Out

Dynamic comedians can embody any number of characters onstage through the act-out technique, and doing so keeps their audiences rapt, not to mention in stitches. The fact that you're having fun and demonstrating (rather than just telling) draws people in and makes them remember you.

* * * * * * ROI TIP *from* STEVE * * * * * *

WE'VE SEEN CLIENTS act out in hilarious ways. In one instance, the CMO of a global automotive company actually became her Greek American mom chastising her when she was twelve. To make matters worse, they were the only Greek family in an otherwise Irish American school district. As the CMO related the struggles of trying to fit in back in her prepubescent years, she shared with us her mother's ranting: "Why do you wear dat denim jeans clothing? Deess izz not how vee dress! Why aren't you wear dee traditional blue and white of dee homeland? Are you don't proud to be Greek? And why you didn't share dee souvlaki I cooked at your friend sleepover? You tink day don't like my food? All day do is eat corned beef or some-teenk?!!"

Her colleagues laughed out loud and, critically, the act out further humanized a very senior executive in front of her direct reports.

In another instance, a junior associate took the "stage" and decided to become his boss, a senior executive who had already performed and was still in the room. In fact, he was just a few feet away from the associate, right in the front row. "Yeah, I'm going to have to ask you to, yeah, work all day Saturday to complete the, yeah, first draft of that whitepaper that's due in, yeah, three months' time. And also, set aside some extra time Sunday because, yeah, I'm gonna need five thousand words by Monday morning. And, yeah, I'll get you my edits within three or four weeks, yeah, after my extended vacation."

Of course, the executive was the sort to easily laugh at himself, so the put-down/act-out combo landed right on the nose. The room erupted in such strong laughter, it actually built and built until it turned into enthusiastic applause. We comics call this phenomenon an "applause break." I've never gotten one.

I take every opportunity, whether onstage or in a client's conference room, to apply the act-out technique in sharing my disdain for United Airlines. I act out the pilot, "This is Captain Cody here in the cockpit." Then I act myself out, responding, "Where else would he be calling from, baggage claim? The cloud we just passed?" Then as the pilot, "I have good news and bad news. The good news, is thanks to strong tailwinds, we'll be arriving a full thirty minutes ahead of schedule. The bad news is the folks at Newark ATC have been forced to close the airport due to weather, so we're being rerouted to Schenectady. Oh, and one other thing. Thank you for choosing United. We know you have other options." And then, back to myself, "Other options? What other options? I'm at thirty-five thousand feet on my way to Schenectady. What options do I have? Put on a parachute and kick open the emergency exit?"

Callbacks

Comedians use the callback technique to build rapport with audiences by creating the warm and cozy feeling of being inside of an inside joke. At Peppercomm, we have learned to build on each other's running jokes at work.

Our internal Microsoft Teams channel is designed to offset the avalanche of emails and enable one-to-one and one-to-many conversations about everything from individual client needs to human resource activities to some facts and figures one of our teammates felt everyone would enjoy and/or learn from. It's designed for this purpose, but it also lends itself beautifully to sharing callbacks with our teammates. Here are two examples:

The Battle of Birkenstock

Last summer, one of our employees known as Robert the Younger (because we had another employee named Robert who happened to be older than RTY) decided to wear a pair of Birkenstocks to the office. *And* he wore black socks. This did not go unnoticed, and sure enough, someone snapped a pic of RTY, posted it on our Teams channel, and asked the burning question: "Who in God's name would wear Birkenstocks in the office?"

One would think someone had just posted that Des Moines has more rats per capita than Manhattan. The pushback on one side, and support on the other, were incredible. All of a sudden we had a Red State versus Blue State civil war erupting between Birkenstock lovers and haters. But, and this is key, it was all done in a very fun, friendly, and collegial way with RTY laughing right along with everyone else.

Now, if the word ever comes up in a random conversation, the Teams channel will once again refight the Battle of Birkenstock. We're not willing to pick a side here one way or the other; we prefer to stay neutral. But why would anyone wear Birkenstocks in a professional office setting?

A Slay Ride

Every six months, our leadership team holds an all-hands meeting to show every staff member our current financial condition. We're not required to do this, but we make it a rule because our culture values openness. Here, that extends all the way down to being transparent about how the business is doing.

During a recent meeting, we were happy to report that our revenue was skyrocketing. As our staff made up of millennials and Gen Zers began smiling and nodding, one of our senior vice presidents looked out at them and declared, "Way to go, people. You slayed, kings and queens!" There was a slight pause of disbelief, and then everyone burst into laughter. Our SVP, a Gen Xer, had picked that moment to surprise everyone with an unexpected punch line. A person born when Carter was president had just busted out a phrase no one over the age of thirty-two had any business uttering. The room was deadass shook, ong.

Like any good comic, our SVP read the room. He knew his audience, so he took a chance on a roll. This fifty-something dazzled us with his impressive Gen-Z vocabulary: glow ups this, cap that, and of course, slay everything. We all reveled in seeing him less as Larry King and more like Zach.

To this day, 90 percent of people in our agency, of all ages, use slay correctly.

KEY TAKEAWAYS

- **Authentic storytelling**

  Always begin with the truth.

  Share your true thoughts, feelings, and opinions.

  Make sure your emotional fullness comes through.

  When in doubt, leave it out.

- **Team building**

  Laugh together while getting to know your coworkers personally.

Share true feelings and opinions to build stronger bonds and trust.

Cheering each other on creates a positive atmosphere.

Experience and accept coworkers' vulnerabilities and imperfections.

- **Presentation skills**

  Read the room: know what is or isn't working and adjust accordingly.

  Make yourself, and not your PowerPoint slides, the star of the show.

  Develop your charisma and your sense of humor simultaneously.

9

IMPROVISATIONAL
COMEDY IN BUSINESS

IN CHAPTER 6, we examined improvisational comedy and some of the skills its best practitioners have. Improv is team comedy, and improv comedians are all team players.

What if every division of your company were loaded with employees that had the art of teamwork so fully mastered? Imagine if your colleagues and you were capable of spontaneous innovative thinking and real-time, on-the-spot collaboration. What kinds of unexpected and strategic breakthrough ideas might materialize in that environment, and how might they improve your organization's top- and bottom-line results?[1]

Let's look again at the key skills of improv: acceptance, building, and teamwork. But this time, we'll focus on their business applications.

ACCEPTANCE

Acceptance in the business world is unfortunately not always accepted. There are still far too many top-down, autocratic cultures that extinguish a creative thought as soon as it's mentioned. We unfriend those types of clients and instead choose to work only with senior management teams that are open and ready to accept acceptance.

Years ago, we had a financial services client who was so demanding and insensitive that, by today's standards, he would be considered downright abusive. His reputation had preceded him, but as our agency was still growing, we decided to make a deal with the devil, a.k.a. this particular CEO. We charged him a substantial retainer, fully expecting a few bumps in the road. We had no idea what a wild ride we would be in for, indeed.

This, shall we say, "difficult" client had engaged us to work with him and other executives in areas such as media training and crisis management. After a few months of hard work, we demonstrated strong measurable results, despite the fact that our entire team was absolutely exhausted from being berated by him on a daily, if not hourly, basis. On one not-so-fine occasion, this executive missed a scheduled appearance on a major business television network to discuss earnings expectations, due to no fault of ours. We weren't in charge of his day-to-day schedule. In fact, the mistake was made by his head of internal communications, who just so happened to be his girlfriend, and is now his wife. He ranted and scolded us, the not-guilty party, for forty-five minutes straight, calling us every name not in this book.

After cooling off for a day or two, we called this special client up to inform him that Peppercomm would no longer be subjecting our people to this type of treatment. We let him know that, going forward, we would be insisting on at least a modicum of respect. This infuriated him, and he screamed directly into the phone, "That's complete and utter bullshit!"

We no longer have a relationship with that man, his wife, or his company, thank God, but this brutal story has become part of Peppercomm folklore. To this day, every once in a while when someone shares a small, innocuous piece of inconsequential new information, one of us will yell, "That's complete and utter bullshit!" The line always gets a big laugh around here.

Acceptance is the key to collaboration. A 2021 study by the Workforce Institute found that 89 percent of the four thousand employees surveyed felt "heard" at work.[2] That's a great number, obviously, but going deeper into the study, 86 percent felt that people in their organizations were not heard equally. This tells us that employees still feel there is some kind of ceiling between them and the top. It gets worse: 75 percent of employees surveyed reported that they did not feel their input was considered in essential areas such as workplace safety, benefits, and requests for time off. A full 40 percent felt their input, though heard, did not lead to anything actionable at work.

A close examination of this data reveals that, although employees technically feel heard, executives are not actually listening in any meaningful way. There is a massive difference between hearing and listening. Employee engagement is about acceptance, taking opinions and ideas into account, and making real changes based on the feedback.

This is certainly an area in which most C-suites need to improve in order to retain their valued employees and keep morale high. How would you feel if, upon being asked to share your opinions and feedback on workplace safety and compensation, you were essentially ignored by those at the top who had solicited your feedback in the first place? "Why did you ask for my feedback if you're not going to use it to effect any kind of positive changes for me?" is a common, recurring theme and a major pain point among businesses in all industries that we see on a near-daily basis.

Acceptance starts with yes.

BUILDING

Building is the act of adding on. Start with yes, and go from there.

★ ★ ★ ★ ★ ★ ROI TIP *from* STEVE ★ ★ ★ ★ ★ ★

AT PEPPERCOMM, we're addicted to "yes, and . . ." to the point where it comes in basically every conversation about every topic. The results are often at first ridiculous, but eventually we get somewhere. Here's a recent example:

Ann: I still haven't heard back from that West Coast client about the budget increase.

Maggie: Yes, and it's been over a month.

Steve: Yes, and if you don't get that budget increased, you'll be gone in a month.

Tara: Yes, and that's the kind of thing we need to put in writing first.

Maggie: Yes, and the budget request has also been in writing for quite some time.

> Steve: Yes, and I'm writing the thirty-day notice as we speak.
>
> Ann: Yes, and guess what client just emailed me with a budget approval.
>
> Maggie: Yes, and all's well that ends well.
>
> Tara: Yes, and, Steve, please stop threatening the partners.

With our clients, however, we take a gentler, and less ominous, tack.

The power of collaboration and the "yes, and . . ." approach led Peppercomm to develop a PR campaign for the Alliance for Lifetime Income (ALI, not to be confused with the self-proclaimed "Greatest of All Time," Mr. Ali). This group of twenty-four insurance companies had a goal: improve the perception of annuities as a retirement vehicle. Make annuities interesting? That's a job even Ricky Gervais would struggle with. On top of that, they asked us to help Americans understand how annuities remove risk from their retirement programs and do it in a fun way. Paging Ricky G!

We didn't have the budget for the fees normally charged by the creator of *The Office*, so we were on our own. We came up with Retire Your Risk, a program that emphasized the risks inherent in life on Earth by spotlighting three death-defying individuals: a stunt driver, a volcanologist (nice work if you can get it—red hot benefits), and a shark whisperer (whose whispers were often not well received ten thousand feet under the sea).

In order to highlight the risks of these three noble professions, we created a virtual reality bus that enabled consumers to experience them firsthand. People would see our bus, try on our VR goggles, and see how tame their lives were by contrast. More importantly, we helped the average American make the connection to remove risks from their retirement years by buying annuities now.

So, who's ready to hop into a shark tank and go for a dive? The line starts here.

---

* * * * * * ROI TIP *from* STEVE * * * * * *

ANOTHER LINE THAT doesn't get as many laughs but won us several awards and drove record sales for a tire manufacturing client is, "Below 44." We were sitting around our client's conference room table trying to brainstorm a way to get Americans to pay attention to inflating their tires during the winter.

We played improv games to see what might lead to an E-ZPass to the solution. In the middle of the "yes, and ..." game, the client CEO said, "Yes, and once the temperature dips below forty-four degrees, you must inflate your tires for safety reasons." I jumped up. "That's it. Let's go online right now and find out when each of the fifty states typically first experiences temperatures below forty-four degrees Fahrenheit." I knew the idea I had was a winner.

On the day that each state's temperature dipped below forty-four degrees (as one might expect, the northern states dip below forty-four first and places like Florida and Hawaii finish last, climate change notwithstanding), we blitzed all local media in that state with safety alerts, urging them to inflate their tires now. This PR campaign,

---

dubbed Below 44, received extensive coverage in each state but also in national print and broadcast media. Most important, the tires rolled off the assembly line like an avalanche in Alaska.

TEAMWORK

Teamwork is essential. Some even claim it makes the dream work.

✳ ✳ ✳ ✳ ✳ ✳ ROI TIP *from* STEVE ✳ ✳ ✳ ✳ ✳ ✳

WE WERE IN a very high-pressure situation. As is so often the case in industries such as PR and advertising, our relationship with a major client was put up for a mandatory periodic review. We were in a position of having to defend award-winning work. If, God forbid, we lost the account, it would impact the entire agency. We're talking potential catastrophe here, so it was all hands on deck.

We traveled to Philadelphia for our one shot to plead our case in person. We had several members of our executive team set to give presentations, and we also brought along several junior members of our staff, including our day-to-day account lead, Rebecca. To make matters worse, Rebecca found herself in the unenviable position of kicking off the entire meeting. She was more nervous than a ninth grader singing the national anthem

THE ROI OF LOL

at Citizens Bank Ballpark. Further exacerbating Rebecca's plight, the rest of us anxious executives were incessantly drilling her with unhelpful and counterproductive tips, such as "Don't forget to smile," "Don't cross your arms," "Make sure to look the president in the eye."

Poor Rebecca looked as though she'd swallowed all the cheesesteaks in Philly. She stood in front of the selection committee, her hands quivering and her forehead shining. I was doing my best to telepathically channel my best FDR: "Come on, Rebecca. The only thing you have to fear is fear itself."

Rebecca stumbled over every other word for about a minute and then decided to call an audible and kicked a punt that would make the Eagles proud. "Maggie has so much insight about this. Maggie, why don't you share what you were telling me earlier?" Thankful that Rebecca hadn't fainted so far, Maggie jumped in and made some very astute comments. Having regained her composure, Rebecca confidently chimed in, "That's a great point, Maggie, and we should also add key market events tied into the client's favorite charity. Let me show you all the chart on slide 4." From there, Rebecca metamorphosed into a monarch butterfly and flapped her wings at just the right points through the remainder of the meeting.

We retained the business, and Rebecca's looking forward to playing kicker for the Eagles next year.

By accepting, building, and working as a unit, we create content as a group we could never create on our own.

FORMS OF IMPROVISATIONAL COMEDY

Short-Form Improv

Developing skills through short-form improv games allows you to isolate what exactly you're trying to learn. We find that so many short-form improv exercises are quite useful in our business dealings. An organization that struggles with content creation? We have them "yes, and . . ." each other multiple times until they learn to brainstorm like the pros. A company where listening is rare and interrupting is commonplace? We drill them on the "One-Word Story" game and highlight where the breakdowns happen, until their minds are open to what their teammates are trying to say.

We had a client that manufactured a wellness device. Don't ask us what a wellness device is; our answer will make you sick. Regardless, our assignment was to provide media training for two nervous engineers (think, super introverted) who had trouble completing a sentence, even when speaking to each other. These two science-y types were assigned by their company's senior management to be the lead spokespeople for the upcoming Consumer Electronics Show (a convention that would make Woodstock look like a company picnic, and did we mention it's in Las Vegas?) and they weren't ready. You know in Penn and Teller, how Teller doesn't talk? These guys were both Teller.

We took these brainy engineers through a series of short-form improv games and reengineered their minds. Suddenly, they settled in; to our great surprise, they both had incredible stories. We then accelerated the training by having them sit together in an imaginary car on their way to Vegas for the show.

We started off with a travel-related prompt and, *zoom*, they were off to the races, whipping through several imaginary speed traps and hairpin curves along the way. These two "yes and . . ."-ed each other over three thousand imaginary miles, and we learned about them and their company all along the way. They shared the message of their brand in terms that even we could understand. Sure, they went off topic at one point when one admitted to having smuggled their girlfriend in the trunk, but it's always the quiet ones, amiright? We think we heard a knock coming from the imaginary back of the imaginary car.

When they actually arrived at the show in real life, they "won" every media interview. Yes, and . . . they even made the Top Products List in *Time* magazine. And you can catch their act every Friday at 8:00 p.m. at the Park MGM, where they now open for Wayne Newton. "Danke schoen, darling, danke schoen . . ."

Long-Form Improv

Long-form improv involves building an actual scene.

In business, we use this form of improv to help companies who are ready to take their external storytelling to new heights. By improvising and guiding one another toward finding the various conclusions in fictional improvised scenes, companies become better at collaborating to share corporate messaging. This can apply to press releases and other mass emails, live interviews with the press or their industry-specific trade publications, and even their television and radio advertising, which is necessarily driven by corporate missions and the messaging thereof.

We also use the lessons learned in long-form improv to adjust our script to ever-changing conditions. Sometimes we throw away the script altogether, as we did in the case of what Steve calls, in homage to the classic *Seinfeld* episode of the same name, "The Soup Nazi."

★ ★ ★ ★ ★ ★ ROI TIP *from* STEVE ★ ★ ★ ★ ★ ★

I WAS HAPPY that I had developed my improvisational skills on the day I had to connect with one of the most egotistical and narcissistic CEOs I've ever had the misfortune to meet.

We had been contacted by a Texas-based software company whose CMO said they'd already conducted due diligence and decided Peppercomm would be their ideal partner. They asked us to put together a sizable program, fly from NYC to Austin, and present our ideas to the megalomaniacal chief executive officer. The annual retainer was a hefty one, so we agreed.

When we arrived in the Lone Star State, the CMO met us in the conference room and told us that Ted, the CEO, had a very important and unexpected meeting with the mayor. As a result, we'd have to cut down our two-hour presentation to forty-five minutes and get right to our "big" ideas.

We agreed and shuffled into the conference room. And we waited. And waited. At long last the CEO's executive assistant came in pushing a cart that contained a large bottle of Perrier, a soup bowl, silver spoon, and a large container of some sort of substance. She proceeded to set the CEO's place setting and ladled a heaping portion of what looked and smelled like gazpacho.

Finally, His Royal Highness arrived.

He sat down and began to slurp his soup. We looked at the CMO with a WTF expression on our respective faces. The CEO glanced up and said, "Proceed with your ideas while I eat. I'll let you know if I have any questions."

This was complete and utter bullshit. (See what I did there? That's what we call a callback.) So I looked the software genius in the eye and said, "You know what, Ted, we flew down late last night in order to meet with you (on our own dime), haven't had breakfast, and are absolutely starved. How about we all have some of that soup and then we'll share our ideas."

What came next was a pause more pregnant than the Old Woman Who Lived in a Shoe. The Soup Nazi put down his spoon, looked at me, and asked, "Do you have any idea how important I am?" I shrugged my shoulders and said, "I know how hungry we are. Why don't we end the meeting now. You finish your soup, and we'll go across the street and order that restaurant's finest bowl of pasta e fagioli. Good luck in your search."

Not used to such pushback, the egomaniacal CEO paused, smiled, called his executive assistant, and told her to fetch five additional bowls for us. He also told her to tell the mayor he'd be late. We proceeded with the pitch and were awarded the business.

By learning the skills of long-form improv, you will gain the confidence to trust your own storytelling abilities and make it up as you go along.

TOOLS OF IMPROV

The First-Best Rule

Every Thursday at Peppercomm, we do something special we call "Food for Thought." We feed our employees in exchange for having them participate in one of our many brainstorming sessions. We brainstorm over lunch on everything from our newest client's immediate challenge (and completely impossible demand) to coming up with a title for a business book to be published by HarperCollins! In fact, with the latter, a team of thirty-plus brainstormers came together to nail down the ideal title. The first idea was, "How about something using LOL?" Immediately, we all began throwing out suggestions that included the acronym, and eventually our senior vice president, Paul Merchan, blurted out, "The ROI of LOL!" As a group, we all knew we'd found a winner.

We always use the First-Best Rule to get things going.

On one memorable occasion, we came together to brainstorm ideas to mark the twenty-fifth anniversary of the first *Teenage Mutant Ninja Turtles* movie, which, along with *Gone with the Wind* and *Citizen Kane*, usually finds its way into the American Film Institute's Top 50 of All Time. We were vying to become the agency of record for the four Italian Renaissance painters, and their favorite reporter, April.

We started this brainstorm off with a turtle-related prompt, the word *green*. The first idea was, "Oooh, let's turn the conference room into a replica of a sewer!" Everyone gave the enthusiastic "Yes!" And they added on a very special "Cowabunga!" because everyone knew that the film itself is set in New York's famously foul underground. Ideas flowed off this first-best one, including serving pizza (the only thing the turtles ever eat) to the client decision makers.

When they arrived at our office, we ushered them into our conference room-turned-sewer, replete with slimy, fake pipes everywhere, ominous and drippy sound effects, and signs like TOXIC WASTE and UNION SQUARE adorning our walls. The conference room was a hellish, underground sinkhole even Beelzebub would have found a bit disconcerting. We threw the best sewer-themed pizza shell-abration ever, and the client was dazzled!

We won the business and delivered like Domino's. We hired four actors to portray the turtles and make media appearances on TV and radio. They also made personal appearances outside of famous NYC landmarks such as Grand Central Terminal, Yankee Stadium, and the Guggenheim Museum. They were the talk of the town and received more camera time than even their animated counterparts on the big screen. We even convinced the mayor to light up the Empire State Building in "turtle green" on the day of the anniversary.

We created such a bond with these reptilian clients that Leonardo even stopped by last week for a slice of pizza before ducking back into the 33rd Street subway.

Starting off any brainstorm with first-best will help you come out of your shell.

The Positivity Rule

In order for the action of a scene to build, flow, and advance, the characters in it need to want to be there.

We also apply this concept to our meetings with clients, prospects, sales forces, or angry mobs that might be picketing outside our offices. Positivity determines the success of these meetings, so we have to keep it top of mind.

In fact, we're playful about it and created the Name Game. Before the start of any session, each of us bets a dollar that the others can't be the first to find a way to inject an SAT word like *zeitgeist, truncated,* or *antepenultimate* into an otherwise matter-of-fact meeting. This game keeps us on our toes and smiling as we try to see who can navigate the business conversation and somehow find a logical way to say, "You know that resonates with the zeitgeist of the moment." We stifle our inner laughs, but it always energizes the rest of the session, especially for whoever wins all those dollars.

Bold Choices

The best improvised scenes feature big risks.

We recently worked with one large professional services firm that was reuniting seventy-five global marketing and communications managers from around the world in (where else?) Disney World. (What is the allure of Mickey, Minnie, et al.? We just don't get it.) This was the first time the managers were getting together in the aftermath of COVID-19. In any event, we were working with individuals who ranged in age from twenty-two to seventy-two. Some had been with the firm for thirty years. Others had joined only thirty days prior. And others had been hired just as the pandemic began. So, in addition to many never having met face-to-face, there was also a significant perception that long-term employees had an inherent career path advantage since they already had established face-to-face relationships with the top decision makers.

Our assignment was to change perceptions, break down silos, and get the group to see each other as colleagues who, while they may come from different age groups and geographies, shared a common goal in excelling in their individual jobs and supporting the mission, values, and purpose of the corporation.

This firm faced a challenge being felt by workforces across all industries. Over the past two years, the firm had hired approximately thirty new people to their sixty-person communications team. The majority of the team had never met each other and were struggling to build connections and a sense of collaboration. At the same time, the organization was facing a considerable amount of change. Legacy employees were resistant to changing old ways of doing things, and new employees were frustrated by a lack of willingness to try new things and openness to creativity. According to a pre-session poll, 30 percent of respondents said they were only "somewhat comfortable" sharing information and ideas across teams, and only 50 percent reported that new ideas were "very well" received internally.

Enter the chief comedy officer!

Peppercomm conducted a half-day interactive work-shop that applied the key skills of improv to speed the path to trust, foster a sense of community, and disrupt traditional patterns of thinking to open minds to new ways to boost creativity, collaboration, and problem-solving. Through a series of interactive workshops, the team indeed opened their minds to ways of working and had some fun along the way.

ONE OF THE best parts of my job is watching business-people lose their inhibitions, allowing their creative minds (rather than their analytical minds) to flourish and lead their progress. Because we never focus our improvisational comedy development sessions on silly games that make corporate professionals uncomfortable, they, in turn, get comfortable.

We like to warm up with a few groupthink games. In a room full of actors and other creative types, you can have them start out crawling on the floor, making animal noises, singing songs they haven't written yet, contorting their faces—the sky's the limit with a group accustomed to theatrical norms. But with corporate groups, I always like to reassure them that whatever they've heard about improvisational comedy training is not going to happen today. I say, "Listen, everyone. Nobody's going to be asked to do anything uncomfortable. We're not going to ask you to try to get the silly type of laughs. We're not trying to find out who the zaniest person among you is. We're here to learn some new skills, but only within your personal boundaries." This little speech of mine always has an effect you might find surprising. After I deliver it, the participants actually lose their inhibitions and start making bold choices.

Whereas trying to drag someone kicking and screaming to an area far outside her comfort zone inevitably results in engaging her strongest defense mechanisms, allaying her fears helps her relax. No longer worried that she'll be asked to "perform," our businessperson opens up and is able to, yes, give a performance, but in a truthful way that is not based on pushing her own boundaries to their limits. Instead, she learns how much progress is possible within her natural comfort zone. Within this growth mindset, the business professional comes out of her shell and takes the types of risks that are (a) needed in order for the games to be successful and (b) absolutely appropriate for a corporate training exercise.

After spending the day with this group, I could see major improvements to the way that they were working as a team. Listening skills were front and center. Acceptance of ideas, even seemingly outlandish ones, became the norm rather than the exception. Their commitment to learning something new, combined with the safe space we created for them to feel comfortable experimenting, resulted in bold choices that made the improv games come to life. By the end of the day, the sense of collaboration and unity were nothing short of palpable.

After our full-day visit, we asked the participants to take another survey, in order to measure progress and results. This time, more than 90 percent of participants reported that the session had opened their mind to new ways of collaborating and contributing with their team, 87 percent reported that the session had helped build trust with their teammates and fostered bonds that will carry into their work moving forward, and more than 80 percent reported that they had learned skills that would help them feel more comfortable sharing opinions and ideas with their internal clients.

One participant commented, "We accomplished more in one five-minute exercise than we have in any hour-long Zoom meeting in the past two years. The connectivity and collaboration were simply awesome!"

Active Listening

Active listening is critically important to any business executive, particularly in a selling situation. It's fundamental to be in full listening mode and wait for the one word or clue that might indicate a customer's want or need that your organization is uniquely qualified to provide. The very best salespeople do this naturally, and just as well as their improv counterparts. But for the rest of us in this dog-eat-dog business world in which we coexist, active listening is a critical skill fundamental to both the individual's and the company's future success.[3]

★ ★ ★ ★ ★ ★ **ROI TIP** *from* **STEVE** ★ ★ ★ ★ ★ ★

BECAUSE I'VE WORKED so hard to learn the art of active listening, I was once able to not only overhear a client's problem but present an immediate solution that quickly morphed into a brand-new service offering.

At the end of a long day, the client's team and mine all met for a well-deserved cocktail. As we imbibed another round of sauvignon blanc, they started opening up about their unresolved problems. One was they didn't feel they had first-person knowledge of what their respective customers felt and thought about a given product.

I jumped in, "Hey, we just happen to have a service offering in which Peppercommers put themselves in the *shoes* of customers and actively enter your retail locations and report back to you about the experience. Critically, we also provide PR solutions to help solve those challenges."

One client put down her vodka soda, looked me in the eye, and said, "Steve, you had me at shoes." This client then hired us for a separate project in which we took a deep dive into five of their most important markets and experienced the good, bad, and ugly of trying to buy their products, and we told them what doesn't work from a buyer's standpoint and how to fix it.

The secret sauce here is that we managed to listen well enough to get the voice of the customer into the conference room. It was the first of many successful outcomes we have had with our Audience Experience service offering.

Active listening also helped Steve save the day once amid a last-minute change of plans.

* * * * * * ROI TIP *from* STEVE * * * * * *
BRENDAN AND TED'S EXCELLENT ADVENTURE

BY WAY OF quick background, we had agreed to deliver a half-day presentation to a company that belonged to the Association of National Advertisers (ANA). Our firm had struck a deal with ANA members to hold free workshops in which we'd discuss various public relations topics. In exchange, and assuming they liked what they'd heard, the member firms would then hire us to handle their PR.

We had one successful session after another. And a very important one was coming up that I'd be leading along with one of our up-and-coming executives I will call Ted Bonkers. But, as is sometimes the case, Ted had a last-minute emergency with an existing client and couldn't attend. This was problematic since the ANA firm had already passed out bios of this coauthor and Ted and were expecting the two of us (and, thanks to the client demand, that was no longer going to happen). So, at the eleventh hour, a different midlevel executive I'll call Brendan Byrne agreed to step in and "be" Ted for the half-day session (which was held in some godforsaken spot halfway between Philadelphia and Pittsburgh).

I arrived on time for the workshop, but Brendan (a.k.a. Ted) was late. So I proceeded to kick off the proceedings and, after about thirty minutes or so, Brendan finally arrived. As he walked into the prospective client's conference room, I announced, "Ladies and gentlemen, please give a big hand to the 'late' Ted Bonkers." Brendan flushed fifty shades of red, took his place next to me on the stage, and I continued.

But there was one very big problem. Brendan forgot that he was supposed to be Ted. So, every time I handed the next part of the presentation over to him, I'd say something like, "Okay, Ted, why don't you talk about best practices for scoring an article in the *Wall Street Journal*," and there'd be complete silence.

> But by actively listening to the guy who wasn't actively listening, I was able to step up and say something to the effect of, "Ted's been known to experience stage fright from time to time, so why don't I handle this part?" After this had happened three or four times, Brendan finally settled down, did a great job with the remaining slides, and, believe it or not, we won a nice project.
>
> Now, years later, whenever I run into Brendan, I always greet him by asking, "So, how's it going, Ted?"

Our friend and M&T Bank Chief Marketing Officer Francesco Lagutaine, whom you may remember from chapter 1, has much to say about active listening:

It goes all the way back to who I am and where I come from. I'm multicultural, that's the cool word these days, right? I was born Italian, but by the time I turned eighteen, I had lived in Egypt, Iran, and Australia. When we arrived in Australia, my parents just dropped me off at school three months into the term. I could barely speak playground English and knew nothing about Australian culture at all! I happened to be the only kid that had jeans and a T-shirt on, in a school of boys rocking shorts and ties. I stood out like a great white shark out of water (they have those Down Under). That was a brutal welcome, right?

I have lived abroad my entire career. You develop a sixth sense for listening, because you immediately need to observe and adapt to the givens in order to survive in these shark-infested waters. You don't just listen to what people tell you; you have to listen to what people tell one another in order to understand the rules of engagement across different cultures and settings.

What today we call active listening is the exact same skill I learned all those years ago on the playground. It helps tremendously in my profession even today. I developed a heightened sense of awareness of the things that people do without thinking, subconscious mannerisms and nonverbal indicators. As it pertains to comedy, I always love the great comedians who have the talent to observe and imitate something people do and then work it into their comedy material. It's just incredibly funny to me, and if I'm being honest, I see just a little bit of my multicultural, chameleon self in them.

A big part of active listening, for me, is understanding the time and place for those who report to me, those on my level, and even my CEO. In the latter case, it's not that he never laughs, it's just an element of respect. I'm intentionally a lot less funny with him. It's about observing and respecting how an individual wants to engage. It's true for engaging up, down, and across the many layers of our whole business. I use humor less whenever I pick up on the fact that someone is just not comfortable with that type of communication. Some in the banking sector are simply not comfortable with joking around at work because finance is serious business, and that's okay by me. It's active listening that enables me to find those cues and adjust accordingly. After all, humor is all about timing, right?

Clearly, Francesco sees the value of active listening. He also knows a thing or two about sensitivity, acceptance, building, teamwork, and storytelling. Plus, he loves making people laugh. Clayton's lucky that Francesco's so successful in the banking world; otherwise Clayton would surely find himself losing stand-up gigs to our favorite Italian Australian Iranian Egyptian American funnyman.

KEY TAKEAWAYS

- **Innovation**

    Make bold choices and take big risks.

    Accept others' ideas and build on them.

    Create a safe space where failure is valued.

    Active listening helps you feel and elicit emotions.

- **Attracting and retaining talent**

    People want to be in an environment where creativity thrives.

    Collaboration builds rapport and morale.

    Running jokes bind us together and create camaraderie.

    Inclusion in the elements of change creates stronger teams.

- **Internal and external storytelling**

    Begin and end with the truth.

Communicate to find creative links between different thoughts.

Tailor your story to connect to the right audience at the right time.

Find original ways to embed improvisational techniques at work.

SKETCH COMEDY IN BUSINESS

IN CHAPTER 7, we learned about sketch comedy and how it can help you learn:

- How to be truthful and compelling in storytelling
- How to get a conversation back on course
- How to display authenticity, empathy, vulnerability, and transparency

In this chapter, we'll focus on the various uses of sketch comedy skills in the boardroom, conference room, and the press room.

KEY SKILLS OF SKETCH COMEDY

As we mentioned earlier, the keys to sketch comedy are thesis, observation, and relatability. Just as comedians and sketch writers apply these skills to their work, businesses can improve their internal and external messaging through a better understanding of them.

We use sketch comedy in a variety of ways at Peppercomm. It helps with our external storytelling efforts, recruitment, and many other areas. The video sketches that we have produced in-house have garnered us attention and awareness that we otherwise couldn't have gotten. By sharing our personalities using this fun and accessible form of comedy, we have differentiated ourselves in a crowded industry, and the results speak for themselves. We've won countless awards for our workplace culture and innovative breakthrough campaigns in the past few months:

Wins

PR Daily's 2023 Top Agencies

Ragan's Best Places to Work 2023

Ragan's Best Client/Agency Team of the Year 2023

PR Daily 2022 Top Agencies

Bulldog Awards: Captain Sandy Yawn Boating Safety Campaign

Crain's NY 2022 Best Places to Work

Ragan Communications Dynamic Do-er: Maggie O'Neill

PRNews Top Women in PR: Jackie Kolek

PRNews Agency Elite Top 100

Finalist/Honorable Mention

PR Daily Digital Marketing & Social Media Awards: Captain Sandy Yawn Boating Safety Campaign

SABRE Awards North America: Trivago Stamford Beach

SABRE Awards North America: Dole Malnutrition Labels

Ragan's Media Relations Awards: Dole Malnutrition Labels

PRNews Platinum PR Awards: Dole Malnutrition Labels
Content Marketing Awards: Captain Sandy Yawn
    Boating Safety Campaign
Ragan's PR Daily Awards: Binance Big Game

We have even built and presented *live* comedy sketches as new business pitches that led to our winning numerous major assignments over the years, including automaker MINI USA, French manufacturing conglomerate Saint-Gobain (https://www.saint-gobain), and even then *Tonight Show* owner General Electric.

★ ★ ★ ★ ★ ★ ROI TIP *from* STEVE ★ ★ ★ ★ ★ ★

WE WERE INVITED to pitch General Electric's Imagination at Work campaign, with one of the goals being to make the stodgy GE look cool to college and university students who might otherwise choose to work for Microsoft, Google, or Apple Computer. We knew we were in the competition of our lives and would be up against the biggest and best PR firms in the world, so we did something completely unexpected.

Employing all of the tactics of sketch comedy, we decided to resurrect Thomas Edison (who founded GE in 1892) and have him run for president on a new third-party platform we called The Imagination Party.

Those of us who were leading the pitch in front of the various C-suite suits set up the premise. We then had one of our minions, who had dressed in historically accurate garb (think velveteen waistcoat with pearl buttons and matching britches) and donned a wig to "become" Edison, stride into the meeting and deliver his announcement that he'd tossed his straw boater in the ring. His speech covered all of the key goals the Imagination at Work campaign asked us to address including a whistle-stop tour of critical GE markets in a train drawn by a GE locomotive engine. The decision makers were beyond dazzled and—as soon as Edison had finished his remarks, bowed, and left the room—hired us on the spot.

Winning business this quickly, in the middle of a presentation, is as rare as being struck by lightning (by the way, we considered including noted lightning enthusiast Benjamin Franklin as Edison's running mate, but he was busy at work proofing the latest edition of *Poor Richard's Almanack* and thus unavailable). Without our creative approach to this pitch, Peppercomm would have been eaten alive by the larger and more established firms, and GE would have pulled the switch on our electric chair faster than you could say, "Haste makes waste."[1]

Leaders have to be able to shift their messaging in volatile times and present it in the best possible light in prosperous times.[2] Many of the business leaders who work with us express worry and trepidation about making connections with customers as well as employees. In a survey of more than forty-four hundred global CEOs conducted by PriceWaterhouseCoopers, 40 percent admitted to thinking their businesses will not be viable in ten years' time.[3] Today's C-suite leader is looking to communicate her brand's history and competitive position as clearly as possible to build a deeper understanding for analysts, investors, and shareholders. She wants to know how to share her company's story and engage with the next tier of customers.

Many of the answers to the pressing questions this executive faces may be found in a very surprising place, the world of sketch comedy.

THESIS

Having a clear message, a specific point of view, is essential in sketch writing. At Peppercomm, we were once invited to an industry conference in which all the attending agencies were asked to present a video about themselves. The purpose of these videos was for each of the leading agencies to get a better understanding of how they might collaborate if one excelled in a certain area, but another did not. Essentially, these were short video sales pitches through which each agency would be putting their proverbial best foot forward.

Our singular goal was to wake everybody up with our video and underscore how very different we were from the mainstream. We knew every other agency in attendance would present a clip of a stiff executive in a pressed wool suit nervously saying, "Here at XYZ, we work hard for our clients. Now I'm going to give you a tour of our office and introduce you to every single employee here on the seventeenth floor." Hoping to avoid a similar snoozefest, we created a no-holds-barred political attack ad against our own firm.[4] We were the hit of the night, and our fake partisan propaganda parody poking fun at Peppercomm pinpoints the particular peck of pickled peppers . . . Oops. We mean, uh, they liked it.

Ever since the other agencies saw that attack ad, we've been receiving requests for the various services we provide. Our self-deprecating comedy sketch led to our receiving multiple subcontracting opportunities and numerous new business leads in the short term. Our thesis was that we're uniquely equipped to generate ideas and content that get attention due to our sharp comedy skills and innovative thinking. In the long term, others in our industry have come to regard us as the home of irreverence, an agency that is willing to take risks that other agencies will not. While much of our work has nothing to do with comedy, humor, video production, or destroying your political opponents with vicious propaganda, making our mark that day has had lasting effects well beyond the laughter it produced.

We take pride in our role as rebels with a cause. In fact, some would say that Steve is quite the iconoclast,[5] but he sees himself more as the John Lennon of PR. You say you want a revolution?

OBSERVATION

Comedy creators notice the elements of a situation that are not obvious to everyone else. They illuminate the point in a variety of hilarious ways, leading us to see things their way.

We referenced the legendary Chilean politician Pablo Neruda's famous quote "Laughter is the language of the soul" earlier in this text, but if Neruda had seen the 2019 TV spots from Peloton, the late South American's soul might be using some choice language of its own. Three points for the first reader who can tell us the Spanish translation of "What were you thinking!"

In the ad, a husband gives his wife a Peloton exercise bike for Christmas.[6] The wife instantly expresses equal parts joy and nervousness about using the state-of-the-art technology in her fitness routine. The internet instantly expressed equal parts shock and outrage over the sexist, body-shaming ad campaign. Katie Way of *Vice* called the spot "a bleak portrait of a woman in the thrall of a machine designed to erode her spirit as it sculpts her quads." The ad campaign was yanked almost immediately under the weight of the criticism, and the agency who produced it has been spinning its wheels ever since.

What Peloton did wrong is obvious now. Hindsight is always 20/20, and we can see that instead of putting themselves into the bicycle shoes of their target audience, Peloton raced to complete the campaign like the final stages of the Tour de France. As we all know, haste makes waste, and in this case, very bad taste.

You have to know your audience and what they'll think of your observations, because, in this day and age, they'll definitely let you know.[7]

In the end, it's a cautionary tale. What began as a well-intentioned ad campaign designed to boost sales around the holidays ended in a doomsday ride for the brand, which would go on to hit many more potholes in subsequent years. A bumpy ride indeed.

RELATABILITY

Years ago, when we were the agency of record for discount apparel giant TJ Maxx, they revealed unceremoniously to us via email that they were considering replacing us. Our contact there used the phrase "playing the field" with regard to entertaining a pitch presentation from a much larger, global agency. Having been thus put on notice, we were encouraged to share a document stating our case for why the retailer should stick with Peppercomm. We did not share a document.

We spent the afternoon writing a sketch based on a 1970s-style reality dating show and called it *A Perfect Match*. Rather than pleading our case as to our ability to compete with larger agencies with bullet points, type fonts, or flowery language, we turned the whole ridiculous ask into a sketch comedy video unlike anything they'd ever seen.[8] They divorced us a few weeks later anyway, despite claiming to have absolutely loved the creativity of our video. Alas, the CFO decided to take our budget and allocate it instead to upgrading TJ Maxx's IT infrastructure. This remains the only instance in recorded history of Peppercomm losing a piece of business to software.

Regardless of that outcome, working on projects like this one brought us all together as a team and allowed us to have a great time at work, despite being asked by a client to grovel at their feet.

We're often asked by clients to help them figure out clever, memorable ways to observe their fiftieth, hundredth, or in one memorable case, four hundredth anniversaries, the aforementioned Saint-Gobain. (The founder of this French *conglomérat* actually built the mirrors at the Palace of Versailles. How about that for an opening act?) Many PR firms and advertising agencies also look to find special ways to commemorate their respective milestones in their corporate trajectory.

In 2010, for example, Peppercomm sought to find the best way to mark our own fifteenth anniversary as a firm. We invited employees at all levels to help us collaborate on the project, and someone suggested a comedy sketch, a fictitious film trailer for a movie that would never actually be made. This promoted an amazing round of brainstorming that culminated in the production of *Fifteen*, a video starring our staff that excerpted and spoofed classic films such as *Star Wars*, *Casablanca*, and *A League of Their Own* while subtly espousing the virtues of our beloved place of business in PR areas such as employee engagement, measurement, and coverage.

This video was sent out in place of a traditional holiday greeting card in December 2011. It received rave reviews across the board from clients, prospects, and potential hires. Since our employees were all the cocreators and stars of this ridiculous sketch, it burst the thermometer in terms of building trust and teamwork (not to mention morale) internally among the troops. The sense of overwhelming pride we all took in the finished product was in no way reflective of the actual end result.[9] That said, it was a runner-up for Best Trailer at the International Greenland Film Festival (not a real thing). Again, this isn't about turning your office space into 20th Century Fox Studios or Netflix; it's about bonding, collaborating, and telling your story in an innovative and impactful way.

Relatability is key to any comic idea, of course, and when it's missing, well, to paraphrase the eighteenth-century Scottish poet Robert Burns, the best laid plans of mice and men can cause an absolute avalanche of criticism on Twitter. Case in point, the luxury fitness brand Equinox decided in late 2022 to swim upstream when all its competitors were going in the opposite direction. To wit, when every other fitness center was pushing to sign up new members whose goals for the new year included getting into shape, Equinox launched an ad campaign titled, We Don't Speak January. They thought it was cool.

Their message was, "It's not you, it's January," calling the month of January "a fantasy, delivered to your door in a pastel colored box. You are not a new year's resolution." In short, they were refusing to accept any new members in the busiest month of the year for any gym company, and the reaction was swift and severe: "No one who actually cares about fitness goes to Equinox. Rich people just have a biological need to waste money," tweeted one user in January. Another added, "Didn't realize a health club would be so vehemently against people trying to improve their health and well-being." Needless to say, Equinox pulled the ad campaign faster than an Olympic sprinter can pull a hammy.

FORMS OF SKETCH COMEDY

Parody

Parody means comedy built around the framework of an existing construct or other preexisting material. The audience's familiarity with the target is typically key to making the joke work. In the *Fifteen* video we just discussed, we spoofed a typical Hollywood movie trailer. We exaggerated elements found in a typical trailer, such as catchy one-liners, quoting rave reviews, and even the ever-so-trite opening, "If you only see one movie this year."

We employed long-form sketch comedy techniques in a parody video we used for promotional purposes and to attract new business.[10] In order to introduce and perhaps differentiate Peppercomm from our closest competitors, we spoofed the familiar tone of shows like *Dateline* and *20/20*

Investigates and followed over-the-top investigative reporter Clayton Fletcher on his mission to uncover Peppercomm's "sleazy underbelly" as only a top-notch journalist could.

The video, however tongue-in-cheek, reflects Steve's belief that there actually is a sleazy underbelly to public relations. Our leading trade publications routinely overlook everything from fraud to CEOs who say one thing and do another, and are just generally, well, sleazy. Our observation and our thesis are very clear from the moment the premise of the video is established.

The other not-so-well-kept secret in public relations is that the elite firms often receive preferential treatment from those same trade publications. The more these firms spend, the more press they receive. Separation of church and state (that is, editorial and advertising) simply doesn't exist in the world of PR trade media, and that is what made this video particularly impactful for those in the know who saw it. We had the guts to subtly call out the bad actors and not see the PR world through rose-colored glasses.

Finally, this video brought our team together in a new way. None of it was actually scripted, but the script was built in progress through improvisational techniques. Clayton reacted honestly to each person his undercover reporter character "interviewed," and the comedy was born in real time and captured by our not-so-excellent camera. Our employees loved sharing it with friends, family, and the occasional stranger on the J train.

Inversion

When a character is presented doing the opposite of what would normally be expected, you're probably in the middle of an inversion sketch.

In business, companies use inversion to create funny commercials and advertising campaigns. A great example is the gecko lizard who represents GEICO. Rather than hopping around and catching flies on his tongue, the mild-mannered reptile spreads the word about low-cost collision coverage. Nobody saw that one coming!

At Peppercomm, we include inversion in our creative thinking. A brainstorm for a client looking for a concept might go down a path like this:

MAGGIE: How about a baseball team?

STEVE: Yes, and the coach is a Zen Buddhist.

CAROLINE: Yes, and when his team loses, he does inspirational quotes.

JACKIE: "We may have lost the game, but we gained enlightenment."

And even though the final PR campaign may end up having nothing to do with baseball or Buddhism, ideas in the brainstorm often lead to something the client ends up loving. The key is to use inversion as a possible tool to mix things up creatively.

★ ★ ★ ★ ★ ★ ROI TIP *from* STEVE ★ ★ ★ ★ ★ ★

I THOUGHT IT would be fun to one day discard my corner office and suit and tie, and exchange jobs with our receptionist, Kelly. I would do her job for the day, and she would do what I do (sit in conference rooms pretending to care, go to the gym, take a nap on the couch, and go home early).

I slipped into Kelly's chair at the reception desk and began coping with a switchboard whose lights rivaled Times Square on New Year's Eve, employees all simultaneously placing lunch orders, and clients announcing themselves to meet with Tim. I began downing a toxic mix of TUMS, espresso, and some prescription painkillers I found in one of Kelly's desk drawers. I was overwhelmed beyond belief: "How do I order lunch, how do I transfer a call, and who the hell is Tim?" And all of this before 11:00 a.m. By the time 4:00 p.m. rolled around, I was ready to roll out, but not before checking Kelly's desk drawer one last time for the road.

By contrast, Kelly reported that she'd just had one of the best days in her two-year career at Peppercomm. She felt revitalized, rejuvenated, and ready to take on whatever the regular CEO decided to throw at her the next day.

He threw her a 15 percent raise.

Exaggeration

Exaggeration is a powerful communications tool in business. The late Tony Hsieh, founder and CEO of Las Vegas–based online retailer Zappos (www.zappos.com), used the exaggeration technique to address backlash to his company's announcement that they were moving to a holacracy. A holacracy is a management style in which traditional functions of managers are eliminated and job titles are replaced by roles that individuals acquire. When this change was first announced, the employees were frantic; 18 percent of the workforce took the next train out of Sin City. They decided this thing that happened in Vegas should stay in Vegas without them! They collected their severance packages on the spot rather than seeing how this holacracy stuff would play out.

Top business media eviscerated Hsieh and Zappos, with *Harvard Business Review* decrying "the latest trend in self-managing teams" as "bossless" and "a naive social experiment that ignores how things really get done" and *Business Insider* predicting failure because "we're social beings, and social issues get in the way of logic sometimes." The latter even went so far as to doubt the sincerity of the move, speculating, "Holacracy at Zappos could be more of a nominal rebranding—or as [MIT Sloan School of Management professor Jan] Klein says, 'window dressing'—than anything else."[11]

In an era when the average CEO under such extreme pressure from all sides would have adopted a bunker mentality, Hsieh took the road less traveled and did the unthinkable: he was funny.

Hsieh collaborated with the "survivors" to produce a hilarious, self-deprecating video spoofing the idea of a holacracy and the disproportionate hysteria surrounding the announcement.[12] Hsieh directed and starred in this employee-produced comedy piece wherein he wakes up from a dream in which the company has fallen into complete chaos, just like the press had predicted it would.

The benefits of this use of exaggeration were immediate:

- It allowed employees a little face time with the boss to work together in a creative setting. Working with the CEO on a mission-critical project is a once-in-a-lifetime opportunity for the average employee. There is no doubt they immediately shared the outcome with family and friends, saying, "My job and my boss are pretty cool."
- It told employees that everything's going to be fine. When faced head-on with change, humans have a bad habit of gravitating to worst-case-scenario thinking. The video's exaggerated "sky is falling" theme demonstrates how irrational that idea is.
- It delivered a strong recruiting message: This is a fun and engaging place to work. Do you want to be part of a culture where innovation lives or not?
- It calmed the fears of supply chain partners, customers, and other businesses who may have thought Zappos was gambling too much with its future and was one dice roll away from going bust. This also quelled unease on Wall Street.

As is always the case, there are two sides to every story. We had a *very* different Zappos experience. By way of background, Peppercomm's business development director had had a series of outstanding conversations with then senior facilitation developer Vanessa Lawson, who had indicated she was ready to sit down and collaborate with us on a multiphased, long-term comedy integration program for Zappos employees at all levels. We were beyond pumped and hopped on the first flight heading west from JFK.

The next morning, we arrived at Zappos HQ with a spring in our step that would make Ginger Rogers blush. This was a big-time chance with a big-name brand, and we were eager to make a great impression and hit the jackpot in Vegas. As soon as we told the receptionist we were scheduled to meet with Vanessa, she told us the latter was unfortunately out sick. Improvising on the spot, we asked if any of her direct reports were in the office. The response was swift and severe: "No." Scrambling, we then asked to speak to Vanessa by phone. We crapped out again: "No."

Seeing the obvious distress on our faces, the receptionist offered us a tour of the office and a signed copy of Hsieh's autobiography, *Happy at Any Cost*. Unhappy at that moment, we gave it one more shot, imploring the receptionist to call Vanessa and reschedule our meeting for the following morning? No dice.

We returned to NYC with our tails tucked between our legs, having wasted a good ninety-six hours of billable time and substantial out-of-pocket expenses on a fruitless trip to Nevada. Our business development director was outraged and sent countless emails and follow-up calls to Vanessa, all of which were met with profound silence.

We'd love to channel Hsieh and make our own hilarious sketch comedy video about our experience dealing with this "fun and creative" company, but we haven't, out of respect for the dead.

TOOLS OF SKETCH COMEDY

Brainstorming

To refresh your memory, a few things to remember in brainstorming are:

- Accept all the creative and wild ideas.
- Build on other participants' ideas.
- Don't criticize other collaborators' ideas.
- Aim for quantity over quality.
- Make the brainstorming session visual.

Premise

The premise is the idea behind the sketch, which your audience should ideally be able to identify within the first few seconds.

* * * * * * ROI TIP *from* STEVE * * * * * *

FOR MANY YEARS, I penned a daily blog called *RepMan*. On most occasions, I shared my views on crisis communication, reputation management, and the like. But as I became more comfortable with using humor in business, I decided to incorporate a little fun into the repertoire.

In an ongoing premise that became very popular with my readers, I delved into the dangerous area of politics through the perspective of my beloved pit bull, Mick. Mick Cody became a political crusader who believed in civil rights for all canines. He was adamant that dogs should have an equal say in areas such as *Roe v. Wade*, the death penalty, and that every street corner should have a fresh, clean fire hydrant. He was elected our nation's first congressdog in 2014. Sadly, his political career came to a barking halt when TMZ raised one leg and leaked a sexting scandal involving a local feline. Mick felt he'd been framed and set up for failure by his rival, Seamus Romney, a.k.a. Mitt's Mutt.[13]

KEY TAKEAWAYS

- **Strong point of view**

  Find a clear opinion and a way to express it.

  Ensure that your message resonates with your audience.

  Have facts to support your viewpoint.

  Create unexpected or ironic ways to share.

- **Connection with authenticity**

  Use characters and plot to find relatable themes.

  Speak the language of your audience.

  Meet your audience where they are.

  Exaggeration leads to messaging going viral.

- **Sensitivity and mindfulness**

  Be in the moment and for the moment.

  Lampoon the expected by doing the unexpected.

  Play with surprising settings and premises.

  Plan the scenario in advance to test your tone.

BOTTOM-LINE RESULTS

THIS BOOK HAS been a lot of fun to write, and we sure hope it's been fun to read, but we're in the business section for a reason. You want to see results, so let's talk about how what we've explored can elevate your organization to new heights of success and happiness.

EMPLOYEE ATTRACTION AND RETENTION

If we had a dollar for every executive who said he wanted to attract the best and brightest (B&B for short), we'd be competing with Branson and Musk to be the first billionaires on Mars. Today's job candidates not only want to work in a forward-thinking environment; they're demanding it. Every C-suite should know that their most important asset is either typing on a laptop or riding up and down a Hudson Yards elevator. Despite the copious amounts of evidence we've presented herein supporting the power of laughter, most leaders have yet to embrace its obvious benefit in the workplace. You can differentiate yourself from them and attract those B&Bs by getting with the times and in touch with your funny bone at work.

ENHANCED CONNECTIVITY, COMMUNICATIONS, AND MORALE

Whether it's a packaged goods company, an accounting firm, a practice of doctors and nurses, a defense contractor, or a coalition of sidewalk fruit stand vendors, comedy makes a difference. We've seen incredible results teaching skills heretofore known only to performing artists to executives and employees at all levels. Barriers and silos that had existed for months, years, or even decades disappeared. Connectivity improved among those who disliked each other or simply didn't want to meet or collaborate with one another. Storytelling skills are elevated and taken to results-producing levels. As for the effect on team morale, the proof is in the pudding. We've won more workplace culture awards than Nadal has grand slams. By practicing the techniques included in this book, you, too, can ace the opposition and be best-in-class in your industry.

ENHANCED WORKPLACE CULTURE

Instead of trying to convince everyone (including yourself) your workplace culture is healthy (we're like a family here; we always have so much fun), use the skills in this book to make it so. For every company that makes the *Fortune* "Most Admired" list,[1] there are a million that don't. If you keep the fundamentals of TOAST front of mind and review the measurables we shared in this text, you'll have everything you need to make a compelling case that you're healthier than any of your competitors (HDL cholesterol levels/restless leg syndrome notwithstanding).

PRESENTATION SKILLS

Statistics show that 75 percent of humans would rather die than speak in public.[2] The what/when/why/how that we've shared in these chapters will help you not only overcome that fear but look forward to the next big speech, new business pitch, or annual budget review with the boss. Communicating effectively, borrowing techniques from the greatest comedians, will allow you to look forward to something that 75 percent of humans fear more than death. No stats available on what percentage of armadillos are worried.

LISTENING SKILLS

Have you listened to a word we've said up until this point? If not, you're in the majority. Most business executives we know are very poor listeners. In these pages, we have shared tenets of comedy that will be the Q-tip to your ear canal. Listening is a lost ark that Indiana Jones himself couldn't find today, but we promise it's more important now than ever. Become an empathetic, vulnerable, active listener and you'll avoid all the snake pits and oversized boulders that work in the modern era will throw at you when you least expect it. Your workplace will be a haven of connectivity and not a temple of doom.

EMPATHETIC LEADERSHIP

Depending on whom you ask, empathetic leaders are either multiplying faster than rabbits or they're disappearing faster than civility in our public discourse (remember when they used to say, "Don't talk about religion or politics?"). Empathy means being open to admitting fault. It means accepting blame when things don't go your way. It means learning from those around you. It means the best idea always wins. It means letting the whole organization celebrate every win. It means even a meanie can change; after all, the end doesn't always justify the means.

TEACHING THE POWER OF DIY

While we'd love to be your strategic partner, we know that hyperinflation, budget concerns, the heightened cost of living, and that new seventy-two-inch flat-screen you just installed may make that impossible. We're hoping that these pages have given you at least a blueprint for how to implement real change in your business. And we're always just a quick phone call away—unless Steve's on an ice climbing trip in Antarctica or Clayton's headlining in Tupelo. Then you're on your own. What did you think DIY stood for anyway?

REINFORCING THE PURPOSE
OF A PURPOSE-DRIVEN ORGANIZATION

There was an 1849-like gold rush to be "purpose driven" at the height of the pandemic. As we've seen, however, more than a few CEOs somehow confused the words *purpose* and *profit* (and profited handsomely as a result). But while their personal net worth glittered, their company's reputations took a beating that even "Iron" Mike Tyson would admire. These despicable gold diggers were called out in public for this, and some were asked by their boards to hitch the first stagecoach headed east. The fourteen-karat brilliance of using comedy is that it enables you to hold your organization accountable for their purpose-driven commitments. While your reason for being may be serious, keep your sense of humor while sharing your purpose as a team, because there's gold in them thar hills!

EMBRACING CHANGE WITHIN THE ORGANIZATION

Nobody wants to change. Getting the average employee to change is harder than getting your phone to cast to your television. (The phone may be smart but we sure aren't. Steve hasn't been able to figure out a single piece of technology since the printing press.) Comedy can be a gateway to easing the tensions that come with the natural resistance to change. It can be your direct message to make change seem more natural and let your organization know WhatsApp! By plugging in to the marketplace and gaining a competitive advantage, you'll do to your competition what the DVR did to television commercials: you'll speed right past them.

USING COMEDY AS A STRATEGIC DIFFERENTIATOR TO EVERY STAKEHOLDER AUDIENCE

Every human being is as unique as a snowflake. Every audience you want to connect with, too, is unique. They may not appreciate the implication of being called snowflakes, so don't do that unless you want the cold shoulder. Winter is coming to those brands that fail to recognize that their target audiences want to have their uniqueness recognized. It makes them feel cozier than a cup of hot cocoa at a ski lodge in Aspen. To differentiate yourself from your competition, you need to make sure your audience gets you, your purpose, your message, and your mission. If you do that, they'll feel cozy and connected to you. Use your unique sense of humor to connect with them or else you'll be left in the cold.

SELF-ASSESSMENT DIAGNOSTICS

IS ANY BOOK worth the parchment it's printed on unless it includes a self-assessment tool that bemuses, befuddles, and bewitches you? We think not! Here's our version of that particular form of torture (please forgive your coauthors; our editor's forcing us to do this part).

- Am I able to laugh at myself?
    Always
    Never
    Depends on if the Mets are mathematically
        eliminated from playoff contention yet

- Am I open to constructive criticism?
    Always
    Never
    Only if it's of someone else and not me

- Do I see the humor in everyday life?
    Always
    Never
    Depends on whether I've been sideswiped by a bus

- Am I a team player?

  Always
  Never
  Actually, there is an *i* in team

- Does your CEO display empathetic leadership?
  Always
  Never
  Depends on how his stock options are doing

- Does your CEO include every layer of the
  organization in decision-making?
  Always
  Never
  Yes, but only six months after the decision's
      been made

- Does your CEO surround herself with the best
  and brightest minds?
  Always
  Never
  Well, I work here, don't I?

- Does your CEO embrace innovative thinking?
  Always
  Never
  Only in regard to that new addition on his
      beach house

- Is your CEO purpose driven?
    Always
    Never
    He gets driven to the office every day in a limo.
        Does that count?

- Does your organization really feel like a family?
    Always
    Never
    A dysfunctional one, sure!

- Is your organization set in its ways?
    Always
    Never
    Our CFO uses an abacus

- Does your organization's culture embrace
  diversity, equity, and inclusion?
    Always
    Never
    Insert the word *begrudgingly* and you got us

- Does your organization's storytelling resonate
  with stakeholders?
    Always
    Never
    The only resonance around here is the
        boss's MRI

AFTERWORD

Breathing New Life into Diversity, Equity, and Inclusion Training

DIVERSITY TRAININGS ARE NOT FAILING; LEADERS ARE

A January 2023 opinion piece in the *New York Times* posed the question "What if diversity training is doing more harm than good?" Before choosing to spend a few minutes engaging the author's ideas, I wrestled with the potentially absurd thinking that brought the article into existence. First, I quickly juxtaposed the word *diversity* with other important trainings across industries. I could not imagine anyone questioning whether increased emphasis on safety training might create more negative than positive outcomes. Similarly, I reasoned that few would dare suggest a reduced focus on client service training at the risk of being met with near ridicule. And what about technology training—the kind that continues to go over the heads of some employees who would absolutely destroy that stupid all-in-one printer/copy/fax machine if they were to ever find themselves in the building undetected and alone? There is no way any manager would seriously entertain the notion to simply stop producing the accompanying instructional sheets, emails, and videos as a method to solve the issue.

Second, I thought about quitting—literally bypassing the article title's frustrating reminder that many of us who champion DEI initiatives have no small number of colleagues who question and/or devalue our efforts. But this would have been too easy. I do not subscribe to the idea that diversity training should necessarily make people uncomfortable; I believe that learning can be fun under the facilitation of creative and resourceful leaders. Yet I do not support the practice of preventing or avoiding the awkward interactions that sometimes arise in DEI discussions.

The *New York Times* opinion piece challenged me to spar with widespread pushback against the evidence that DEI initiatives can make work environments more productive. It communicated the idea that diversity training that "threatens dominant groups' sense of belonging or makes them feel blamed may elicit negative backlash or exacerbate biases." Unfortunately, this rationale is rooted in logic that presumes a problematic dichotomy from the start. Effective diversity training should center on togetherness—the strength of the whole when all team members feel safe, welcomed, and valued. But how?

The most helpful starting point for leaders responsible for improving workplace climates is understanding the meanings of diversity, equity, and inclusion and properly inserting them as meaningful components of a successful work culture.

Diversity refers to variety and the differences therein. Employee diversity can cross many categories, including country of origin, family and ethnic background, race, sex, age, culture, professional background and training, religious or political beliefs, and personality.

Equity refers to the existence of policies, practices, and institutional messages that work to eliminate unfair differences in outcomes. The end goal is for all team members to enjoy the opportunity to improve their lives devoid of gaps in opportunity and resources.

Inclusion refers to the value and practice of genuinely welcoming traditionally excluded individuals and/or groups into processes, activities, and decision/policy making in a way that shares power.

There are additional core definitions that should be added to a brief diversity introduction/language guide (please do not make people take quizzes!) to establish common understanding.

LEADERSHIP REQUIRES ACTION

When faced with challenges, effective leaders move from understanding to commitment to action. More employees will be motivated to embrace the value of diversity in the workplace when they see genuine investment from those in the C-suite, and this improvement in culture can happen even more readily if leaders develop a clear, definitive program of the "how." The central idea of this book is that the "how" should include laughter.

Leadership involves change. Team members across industries are willing to be challenged in new ways, and leaders driving change should be equipped with new knowledge, new tools, and new courage. Not because they have to but because they want to—the difference is easily recognizable.

DEI works best when there is a cross section of leaders and teams that combine to form a critical mass that realizes the benefits of diversity in the organization. When people from historically disadvantaged groups feel seen, heard, and valued in the workplace, the likelihood of that work environment achieving measurable gains is increased.

EGGSHELLS AND EGGHEADS ARE BAD FOR BUSINESS

Recently, an African American woman in a large organization reached out and shared her refusal to speak during her team's biweekly diversity sessions. The woman's self-imposed silence centers on the potential consequences, including the derailment of her career, for speaking openly and honestly. If she were to explain to her fellow team members and managers that their response to the murder of George Floyd has proven more performative than genuine, and that previous calls for greater attention to DEI well before Floyd's murder were ignored or dismissed, would she not be labeled as problematic or "not a team player"? As the only person of color on her team, the African American woman has given false responses for over two years on surveys that purport to measure the DEI climate within her organization. The mandatory pre-survey demographic questions (for example, length of time with the company, remote work status) make it easy to determine her identity.

Leaders with deep vocabularies might call this a conundrum, but I prefer to recognize it as a hot mess. We should seriously consider how many people across industries who want to improve their work environments are instead fearful of their thoughts being unwelcomed or attacked. Sadly, despite biweekly opportunities to voice questions and concerns in diversity sessions, the African American woman in the current example feels so unsafe that she continues to mask her frustrations and concerns.

Leaders must understand that many people from historically disadvantaged groups can enter diversity sessions with little interest in and incentive for being fully present. Their reluctance is often tied to executives' strategy of "volun-telling" people from historically disadvantaged groups to lead the company's diversity efforts and, as is often the case, speak on behalf of their disadvantaged group. Umm, sick day, please? Muslim team members should not be responsible for educating their coworkers about Islam and making them feel comfortable with potential business partners who share their faith. If individuals from disadvantaged groups are not being given a choice and compensation for the added responsibility of diversity work, it can be particularly harmful to team morale.

Leaders establish the identity of the group. In this regard, diversity trainings are not failing; leaders are. A helpful lesson that leaders can learn from comedians is the art of establishing oneness with an audience. When common communication barriers between executives and employees are removed, it helps create an environment of trust and cooperation. This is the point at which effective diversity trainings should begin.

In a healthy work culture, an African American woman should feel safe to identify the failures of her organization's response to demonstrate its stated DEI values. Muslim employees should not feel pressured into attending and leading diversity sessions primarily because of their religion. It is an effective leader's responsibility to build a climate that makes all team members feel understood or important enough that leaders are invested in achieving understanding. Again, the premise of this book is that humor should be a part of these communications and larger processes.

While laughter is an effective tool in diversity trainings, its use is not intended to make fun of anyone's race, gender, religion, sexuality, ability, or national origin. For example, when humorous self-deprecation is used as a tool in building positive working relationships within an organization, it should never be coupled with comparison to any specific team members or people in their larger disadvantaged group.

For leaders who wish to engage their teams in a diversity discussion that is sure to include laughter, consider an old West African practice. Chiefs would occasionally host public gatherings and allow village members to make fun of their stewardship. (Some believe this is the origin of "the dozens," a verbal comedy sparring contest popular in African American communities.) In today's world, this practice can be modified and coupled with technology to promote team building and diversity awareness at once.

To get started, give team members time to anonymously share thoughts on DEI in the workplace from your perspective. Encourage exaggeration. Next, use Comic Life 3 to create a magazine using your facial expressions to demonstrate team members' assessments. Present the finished product to your team during its next diversity session. Note that some anonymous notes received may need to be filtered out of the magazine that's created, but your funny introduction using the magazine will have brought the team together in laughter and made possible an easier transition to discussing a concerning submission or other business. Plan your "performance" ahead of time as much as possible, but keep in mind the probability of needing to just go with it!

Unfortunately, many leaders and participants in today's DEI trainings are either checking a box or faking enthusiasm to protect their positions. If more leaders focus on creatively constructing the "how" to make these sessions more genuine, efforts are likely to become more meaningful.

One large organization recently placed a moratorium on the use of DEI policies in its hiring practices, arguing that positions filled using criteria other than merit result in reduced organizational effectiveness. First, the term *diversity hire* is incredibly offensive to individuals from disadvantaged backgrounds who meet or exceed the requirements of their roles. Second, this type of attack against DEI policies in hiring practices rejects the notion that a workforce reflective of the ideals of diversity, equity, and inclusion is merit worthy. It is quite apparent, then, that far more diversity training is needed, not less. And if more leaders leverage humor in mediating the current divide, more people will "get it." But, please, not without laughter.

RESOURCES

Articles

American Marketing Association—Jennifer Murtell, "Anticipating the Future of Generational Insights," January 23, 2020, https://www.ama.org/marketing-news/anticipating-the-future-of-generational-insights/. Discusses the blanket tastes of the boomer generation, Gen X, and millennials. Covers self-deprecation.

American Psychological Association—Brad Bitterly, Alison Wood Brooks, and M. E. Schweitzer, "Risky Business: When Humor Increases and Decreases Status," https://psycnet.apa.org/doiLanding?doi=10.1037%2Fpspi0000079.

CNBC—Vicky McKeever, "Why Laughter Can Make You More Productive at Work," July 8, 2021, https://www.cnbc.com/2021/07/08/why-laughter-can-make-you-more-productive-at-work.html.

EBN—Deanna Cuadra, "Can Laughter Be an Employee Benefit? This Company Is Making It Possible," November 30, 2022, https://www.benefitnews.com/news/why-laughter-may-be-an-essential-employee-benefit.

Economist—"It's the Real Thing," November 14, 2015, https://www.economist.com/business/2015/11/14/its-the-real-thing. Authenticity as an important quality for a brand, according to millennials surveyed.

Fast Company—Jennifer Aaker and Naomi Bagdonas, "Humor Is Such an Important Leadership Trait We Teach It at Stanford's Business School," January 26, 2021, https://www.fastcompany.com/90597762/humor-is-such -an-important-leadership-trait-we-teach-it-at-the -stanford-b-school.

Forbes—Bryan Robinson, "Comedy's New Role in the Work-place, Replacing the Dreaded Happy Hour," November 10, 2022, https://www.forbes.com/sites/bryanrobinson/2022 /11/10/comedys-new-role-in-the-workplace-replacing -the-dreaded-happy-hour/?sh=5cd800263665.

Forbes—Mark Johnson, "Three Ways to Make Fun of Your-self at Work and Win," September 17, 2021, https://www .forbes.com/sites/forbestechcouncil/2021/09/17/three -ways-to-make-fun-of-yourself-at-work-and-win/?sh =5a18f89a16b7.

Forbes—Shep Hyken, "A Little Laughter Decreases Stress and Improves Productivity," September 5, 2021, https://www.forbes.com/sites/shephyken/2021/09 /05/a-little-laughter-decreases-stress-and-improves -productivity/?sh=75e6a60936d6.

Harvard Business Review—Jennifer Aaker and Naomi Bagdonas, "How to Be Funny at Work," February 5, 2021, https://hbr.org/2021/02/how-to-be-funny-at-work.

Inc.—Tim Crino, "Comedian Sarah Cooper's Top Rule for Humor at Work: 'Don't Try to Be Funny,'" https://www .inc.com/tim-crino/sarah-cooper-jennifer-aaker-naomi -bagdonas-humor.html.

Insperity—"Humor in the Workplace: What's Funny, What's Not," https://www.insperity.com/blog/humor-in -the-workplace/.

LSE Business Review—Teresa Almeida and Cecily Josten, "Not a Joke: Leveraging Humour at Work Increases Performance, Individual Happiness, and Psychological Safety," https://blogs.lse.ac.uk /businessreview/2021/04/28/not-a-joke-leveraging -humour-at-work-increases-performance-individual -happiness-and-psychological-safety/.

Men's Journal—Erin Alexander, "Being Funny at Work Could Get You a Raise: the Do's and Don'ts of Office Humor, May 21, 2018, https://www.mensjournal.com /health-fitness/being-funny-work-could-get-you-raise -dos-and-donts-office-humor.

New York Times—Corinne Purtill, "How to Laugh at Work," March 6, 2021, https://www.nytimes.com/2021/03/06 /business/dealbook/humor-seriously-work.html.

Next Avenue—Michelle Wojciechowski, "What's Funny at Work These Days?" July 28, 2021, https://www .nextavenue.org/office-humor-jokes-at-work/.

QSR magazine—Sam Oches, "The Many Acts of Domino's Pizza," August 2010. Discusses the self-deprecating re-brand of the company and how it helped profits, https:// www.qsrmagazine.com/menu-innovations/many -acts-dominos-pizza.

Real Leaders—Zina Sutch and Patrick Malone, "What Jerry Seinfeld Taught Me About Employee Engagement," https://real-leaders.com/what-jerry-seinfeld-taught-me -about-employee-engagement/.

SECURITY Magazine—Michael Gips, "Humor in Leader-ship? Funny You Should Ask," March 3, 2021, https:// www.securitymagazine.com/articles/94742-humor-in -leadership-funny-you-should-ask.

SHRM—Stephanie Vozza, "How Managers Can Use the Rules of Comedy to Engage Teams," September 8, 2021, https://www.shrm.org/resourcesandtools/hr-topics/people-managers/pages/how-managers-use-comedy-.aspx.

Social Media Today—Jose Angelo Gallegos, "How Self-Deprecating Advertising Creates More Meaningful Consumer-Brand Connections," March 7, 2018, https://www.socialmediatoday.com/news/how-self-deprecating-advertising-creates-more-meaningful-consumer-brand-con/518531/.

Stanford Graduate School of Business—Joel Stein, "This Is Not a Joke: The Cost of Being Humorless," January 28, 2021, https://www.gsb.stanford.edu/insights/not-joke-cost-being-humorless.

Stanford Graduate School of Business—Kelsey Doyle, "Class Takeaways: Humor Is Serious Business," November 1, 2021, https://www.gsb.stanford.edu/insights/class-takeaways-humor-serious-business.

Travel + Leisure—Stacey Leasca, "Having a Sense of Humor Could Add 8 Years to Your Life and Lead to a Better Career," February 20, 2021, https://www.travelandleisure.com/trip-ideas/yoga-wellness/humor-can-add-years-to-your-life-better-boss.

Wall Street Journal—Rachel Feintzeig, "How to Be Funny—Not Offensive—at Work," February 21, 20921, https://www.wsj.com/articles/how-to-be-funnynot-offensiveat-work-11613955600.

Wiley Online Library—Laura E. Kurtz and Sara B. Algoe, "Putting Laughter in Context: Shared Laughter as Behavioral Indicator of Relationship Well-Being," https://onlinelibrary.wiley.com/doi/abs/10.1111/pere.12095.

Books

Humor, Seriously: *Why Humor Is a Secret Weapon in Business and Life (And how anyone can harness it. Even you.)* by Jennifer Aaker and Naomi Bagdonas.

Shtick to Business: *What the Masters of Comedy Can Teach You About Breaking Rules, Being Fearless, and Building a Serious Career* by Peter McGraw.

Businesses—April Fools' Day Campaigns

General Electric—What's the Matter with Owen BBDO New York, https://www.youtube.com/watch?v=wJZHX fcNZBU.

Google Introduces Screen Cleaner, https://www.youtube .com/watch?v=YYlDb-opAvo.

LEGO "SmartBricks," https://twitter.com/LEGO_Group /status/1377516169813499909.

Tinder Introduces Height Verification, https://twitter.com /Tinder/status/1111721002629660673?.

UNO Pizzeria & Grill Says Goodbye to Deep Dish Pizza, https://www.prnewswire.com/news-releases/uno -pizzeria--grill-says-goodbye-to-deep-dish-pizza -301260087.html.

Velveeta Announces New, "Creamy" Skin-Care Products, https://vbyvelveeta.com/fbsweeps/sweeps/VbyVelveeta.

Businesses—Super Bowl Commercials

Apple TV+—Everyone but Jon Hamm, https://www.youtube .com/watch?v=VD3wy3drkyA.

Booking.com—Idris Rehearses for Big Game Debut, https:// www.youtube.com/watch?v=CWbmcw_GFbU.

Leaders

Harvard Kennedy School's Institute of Politics—John F. Kennedy's Wit and Humor, https://www.youtube.com /watch?v=Ua8HCwDvcK0.

Jack Ma—Keynote Speech at Gateway Canada, https:// www.youtube.com/watch?v=A5Wvy9WOxwU.

Jokes from the Pope, https://www.youtube.com/watch ?v=VIPTdtEvr40.

Margaret Edson—2008 Smith College Commencement Address, https://vimeo.com/1085942?embedded=true& source=vimeo_logo&owner=471092.

The Obama White House—President Obama Speaks at the White House Correspondents' Association Dinner, https://www.youtube.com/watch?v=l-5vD5YVLv8.

Reagan Foundation—The Best of President Reagan's Humor, https://www.youtube.com/watch?v=Pgs-LaWyUJI.

Senator Elizabeth Warren—How She Would Defend Marriage Equality at the CNN Equality Town Hall, https:// www.youtube.com/watch?v=lr8-Ln3FK64&t=4s.

Tony Fernandes—Know Your Stuff and People, Nordic Business Forum 2014, https://www.youtube.com /watch?v=AdyplGlHkwQ&t=71s.

Podcasts

American Psychological Association—Speaking of Psychology: What Makes Things Funny? with Peter McGraw, PhD, https://www.apa.org/news/podcasts/speaking-of -psychology/humor-theory.

Harvard Business Review—How Many Managers Does It Take to Change a Lightbulb? https://www.apa.org/news /podcasts/speaking-of-psychology/humor-theory.

NPR—The Power of Humor, https://www.npr.org/2021 /02/08/965572857/the-power-of-humor.

Peppercomm—Episode 11: Putting Smiles Back on People's Faces, https://laughingmatters.buzzsprout .com/1767584/9887871-episode-11-putting-smiles-back -on-people-s-faces.

Stand-Up

Aparna Nancherla—What It's Like to Live with Anxiety and Depression, Comedy Central Stand-Up, https://www .youtube.com/watch?v=AcslSsWQ3No.

Gary Gulman—Meltdown in Trader Joe's, Comedy Central Stand-Up, https://www.youtube.com/watch?v=j5BZv VlZTyE.

Kenice Mobley—Stand-Up: Keeps Getting Compared to Harriet Tubman, *The Tonight Show*, https://www .youtube.com/watch?v=zuCeTLi0yE0.

TED Talks

A Theory of Everything—Emily Levine (2002). Philosopher-comedian Emily Levine talks (hilariously) about science, math, society, and the way everything connects, https://www.ted.com/talks/emily_levine_a_theory_of _everything?referrer=playlist-the_funniest_ted_talks.

I Got 99 Problems . . . Palsy Is Just One—Maysoon Zayid (2013), https://www.ted.com/talks/maysoon_zayid_i _got_99_problems_palsy_is_just_one?referrer=playlist -the_funniest_ted_talks.

Inside the Mind of a Master Procrastinator—Tim Urban (2016). Tim Urban knows that procrastination doesn't make sense, but he's never been able to shake his habit, https://www.ted.com/talks/tim_urban_inside_the_mind

_of_a_master_procrastinator/c?referrer=playlist-the
_funniest_ted_talks.

Nerdcore Comedy—Ze Frank (2004). Performer and web
toymaker Ze Frank delivers a hilarious stand-up routine,
https://www.ted.com/talks/ze_frank_nerdcore_comedy
?referrer=playlist-the_funniest_ted_talks.

Why Great Leaders Take Humor Seriously—Jennifer Aaker
and Naomi Bagdonas (2021). There's a mistaken belief
in today's working world that leaders need to be serious all the time to be taken seriously. The research tells
a different story, https://www.ted.com/talks/jennifer
_aaker_and_naomi_bagdonas_why_great_leaders_take
_humor_seriously/c.

Websites
QuestForHumor.com—Mary Kay Morrison.

STEVE CODY & CLAYTON FLETCHER

Interviews/Media Hits

Humor That Works—Humor Talks: The Comedy Experience with Peppercomm, https://www.youtube.com
/watch?v=FCSwH9HK7cI.

Inc.—April Joyner, "Why Learning to Tell Jokes Is
Good for Business," https://www.inc.com/magazine
/201110/why-learning-to-tell-jokes-is-good-for-business
.html.

MSNBC Your Business—MSNBC Explores "Humor in the
Workplace" with Peppercomm, https://www.youtube
.com/watch?v=7p6VoznVOtU.

Wall Street Journal—Sue Shellenbarger, "How to Build Instant
Rapport in an Interview," November 29, 2016, https://

www.wsj.com/articles/how-to-build-instant-rapport
-in-an-interview-1480436936.

WNBC—WNBC Profiles Peppercomm's Use of Comedy in
the Workplace, https://www.youtube.com/watch?v
=kPB9UPQ7xpE.

Speaking Engagements

Steve Cody and Clayton Fletcher at Workforce Live, https://
www.youtube.com/watch?v=tDT0EnyKj5E.

STEVE CODY

Interviews / Media Hits

The INBOUND Studio—Steve Cody on the Power of Humor,
https://www.youtube.com/watch?v=vE973ipkVPI.

New York Post—Vicki Salemi, "How Humor Could Help
You Move Ahead in Your Career," June 27, 2021, https://
nypost.com/2021/06/27/how-humor-could-help-you
-move-ahead-in-your-career/.

Wall Street Journal—Barbara Haislip, "What Startups Can
Learn from Improv Comedy," April 25, 2019, https://
www.wsj.com/articles/what-startups-can-learn-from
-improv-comedy-11556206638.

You Can't Laugh at Work 1—Stand Up to Traditional Leadership Ft. Steve Cody of Peppercomm, https://www.youtube
.com/watch?v=KqSE6bw5wXo.

Podcasts

Association of National Advertisers—Champions of Growth
podcast, "Using Comedy in Marketing and Advertising,"
January 19, 2022, https://www.ana.net/miccontent/show
/id/pod-2022-01-growthc-using-comedy-in-marketing.

Stand-Up

"Steve Cody at NYCC January 21 2011," https://youtu.be /UUqpk_sLRYY.

YouTube channel, https://www.youtube.com/user /repmancomedy.

CLAYTON FLETCHER

Interviews/Media hits

Wall Street Journal—Sue Shellenbarger, "The Joke That Makes or Breaks You at Work," January 24, 2017, https:// www.wsj.com/articles/the-joke-that-makes-or-breaks -you-at-work-1485273069.

Stand-Up

"Color Blind—Clayton Fletcher (Stand Up Comedy)," https://www.youtube.com/watch?v=v70eSAAtJ_w.

YouTube channel, https://www.youtube.com/channel /UCjxrqMGV-YIrGmmqkK6uTaA.

NOTES

1: Introduction: The Need for Laughter in an Uncertain World

1. Daniel Smith, "Medieval Jesters—And Their Parallels in Modern America," *History Is Now Magazine*, https://www.history isnowmagazine.com/blog/2019/1/13/medieval-jesters-and-their -parallels-in-modern-america.

2. David Covucci, "Elon Musk Accused of Going Back to His 'Apartheid Roots' After Losing Twitter CEO Vote, Proposing Poll Tax," Daily Dot, December 20, 2022, https://www.dailydot .com/debug/elon-musk-poll-tax/.

3. "How Fox & Robin is Using Gen Z's Absurd Humor to Stand Out—and Go Viral," YPulse, December 1, 2022, https://www .ypulse.com/article/2022/12/01/how-fox-robin-is-using-gen-zs -absurd-humor-to-stand-out-and-go-viral/.

4. Shirin Ghaffary, "Elon Musk Can't Take a Joke," Vox, November 16, 2022, https://www.vox.com/recode/2022/11/16/23461217/elon -musk-twitter-fired-employees-free-speech-contradictions-joke.

5. Nicholas Gordon, "Musk Suggests Major Change to Twitter Polls After Voters in the Last One Told Him to Step Down as CEO," *Fortune*, December 20, 2022, https://fortune.com/2022/12/20 /elon-musk-loses-twitter-poll-blue-votes-ceo/.

6. Michael Sainato, "'Coffee-Making Robots': Starbucks Staff Face Intense Work and Customer Abuse," *The Guardian*, May 26, 2021, https://www.theguardian.com/business/2021/may/26/starbuck -employees-intense-work-customer-abuse-understaffing.

7. David Streitfeld, "How Amazon Crushes Unions," *New York Times*, March 16, 2021 (updated October 21, 2021), https://www .nytimes.com/2021/03/16/technology/amazon-unions-virginia.html.

8. Sarah Bedrick, "How to Reduce Worker Turnover at Your Restaurant, Coffee Shop, or Fast Food Chain," Compt, n.d., https://

www.compt.io/hr-articles/how-to-reduce-worker-turnover
-at-your-restaurant-coffee-shop-or-fast-food-chain.

9. Edward Segal, "Amazon Responds to Release of Leaked Documents Showing 150% Annual Employee Turnover," *Forbes*, October 24, 2022, https://www.forbes.com/sites/edwardsegal /2022/10/24/amazon-responds-to-release-of-leaked-documents -showing-150-annual-employee-turnover/.

10. "M & T Bank Reviews," Glassdoor, https://www.glassdoor.com /Reviews/M-and-T-Bank-Reviews-E858.htm.

11. "M&T Bank Employee Job Reviews in the United States," CareerBliss, n.d., https://www.careerbliss.com/mt-bank /reviews/#:~:text=On%20average%2C%20employees%20 at%20M%26T,an%20average%20rating%20of%204.8.

2: Peppercomm's History with Comedy Training

1. "MSNBC Explores 'Humor in the Workplace' with Peppercomm," Peppercomm, YouTube video, February 11, 2011, https:// www.youtube.com/watch?v=7p6VoznVOtU.

2. "Fastco: The Business Case for Getting Your Team to Laugh Together," Peppercomm, May 12, 2022, https://www.peppercomm .com/fastco-the-business-case-for-getting-your-team-to-laugh -together/.

3. Vicki Salemi, "How Humor Could Help You Move Ahead in Your Career," *New York Post*, June 27, 2021, https://nypost .com/2021/06/27/how-humor-could-help-you-move-ahead-in -your-career/.

4. "Best Places to Work 2012: Peppercomm Inc.," *Crain's New York Business*, n.d., https://www.crainsnewyork.com/awards /peppercomm-inc.

3: The Power of Laughter

1. Brandon M. Savage, Heidi L. Lujan, Raghavendar R. Thipparthi, and Stephen E. DiCarlo, "Humor, Laughter, Learning, and Health! A Brief Review," *Advances in Physiology Education* 41, no. 3 (2017), 341–347, https://doi.org/10.1152/advan.00030.2017.

2. Stephanie Watson, "Oxytocin: The Love Hormone," Harvard Health Publishing, July 20, 2021, https://www.health.harvard .edu/mind-and-mood/oxytocin-the-love-hormone.

3. Katey Davidson, "Why Do We Need Endorphins?" Healthline, July 12, 2017 (updated November 30, 2021), https://www.healthline.com/health/endorphins.
4. Joshua Glawson, "How Comedy, Laughter, and Humor Can Improve Your Life," FEE Stories, January 4, 2023, https://fee.org/articles/how-comedy-laughter-and-humor-can-improve-your-life/.
5. Harriet Taylor, "EHarmony CEO: The Ingredient Online Dating Sites Could Be Missing About Attraction," CNBC, April 2, 2017, https://www.cnbc.com/2017/03/31/eharmony-ceo-online-dating-is-missing-humor.html.
6. Lucia Maffei, "This Dating App Finds a Match Based on Your Sense of Humor," *Boston Business Journal*, February 8, 2022, https://www.bizjournals.com/boston/news/2022/02/08/this-dating-app-finds-a-match-based-on-your-sense.html.
7. University of Kansas, "Laughter, Then Love: Study Explores Why Humor Is Important in Romantic Attraction," ScienceDaily, September 3, 2015, https://www.sciencedaily.com/releases/2015/09/150903131553.htm.
8. "Laugh It Up: Why Laughing Brings Us Closer Together," *PsychAlive*, n.d., https://www.psychalive.org/laugh-it-up-why-laughing-brings-us-closer-together/.
9. Chris Burslem, "Have You Heard the One About . . ." The Big Story, Instore Mag, July 28, 2022, https://lsc-pagepro.mydigitalpublication.com/publication/?m=13436&i=750908&p=30&ver=html5.
10. Peter Farb, "Speaking Seriously About Humor," *Massachusetts Review* 22, no. 4 (Winter 1981), 760–776, https://www.jstor.org/stable/25089220.
11. Teresa Almeida and Cecily Josten, "Not a Joke: Leveraging Humour at Work Increases Performance, Individual Happiness, and Psychological Safety," LSE Business Review, April 28, 2021, https://blogs.lse.ac.uk/businessreview/2021/04/28/not-a-joke-leveraging-humour-at-work-increases-performance-individual-happiness-and-psychological-safety/.
12. Jill Suttie, "How Laughter Brings Us Together," *Greater Good Magazine*, July 17, 2017, https://greatergood.berkeley.edu/article/item/how_laughter_brings_us_together.
13. N. Lehmann-Willenbrock and J. A. Allen, (2014). "How Fun Are Your Meetings? Investigating the Relationship Between Humor Patterns in Team Interactions and Team Performance," *Journal*

of Applied Psychology 99, no. 6 (2014), 1278–1287, https://doi
.org/10.1037/a0038083.

4: Five Characteristics of a Healthy Workplace Culture

1. Kristin Martic, "Building a Positive Workplace Culture: Importance and Best Practices," Haiilo, January 8, 2023, https://haiilo
.com/blog/positive-workplace-culture-benefits-best-practices/.
2. Caroline Rosenberg, Arlene Walker, Michael Leiter, and Joe
Graffam, "Humor in Workplace Leadership: A Systematic Search
Scoping Review," *Frontiers in Psychology* 12 (2021), https://www
.frontiersin.org/articles/10.3389/fpsyg.2021.610795/full.
3. Jeff Dyer, Nathan Furr, Curtis Lefrandt, and Taeya Howell,
"Why Innovation Depends on Intellectual Honesty," *MIT Sloan
Management Review*, January 17, 2023, https://sloanreview.mit
.edu/article/why-innovation-depends-on-intellectual-honesty/.
4. Boris Ewenstein, Wesley Smith, and Ashvin Sologar, "Changing Change Management," McKinsey, July 1, 2015, http://www
.mckinsey.com/featured-insights/leadership/changing
-change-management.
5. Sally Percy, "Why Do Change Programs Fail?" *Forbes*, March 13,
2019, https://www.forbes.com/sites/sallypercy/2019/03/13
/why-do-change-programs-fail/?sh=567a810d2e48.
6. Sara L. Johnson, "Authentic Leadership Theory and Practical
Applications in Nuclear Medicine," *Journal of Nuclear Medicine Technology* 47, no. 3 (September 2019) 181–188, https://tech
.snmjournals.org/content/47/3/181.
7. Chris Melore, "Nearly Half of Americans Turn Camera Off
During Zoom Meetings Over Appearance Insecurities," Study-
Finds, August 12, 2021, https://studyfinds.org/skin-care-zoom
-meetings/.
8. "Trivago CEO's Son Crashes CNN Interview," Quest Means Business, YouTube video, January 25, 2021, https://www.youtube
.com/watch?v=n-Rvm5RblJ4.
9. Hal Koss, "7 Leadership Lessons from Former Netflix CEO
Reed Hastings," Built In, January 20, 2021, https://builtin.com
/company-culture/netflix-book.
10. Jennifer Murtell, "Anticipating the Future of Generational Insights," American Marketing Association, January 23, 2020,

https://www.ama.org/marketing-news/anticipating-the -future-of-generational-insights/.

11. Kyle Johnson, "Jim Belushi Wants You to Know That the 2019 Ford Transit Connect Wagon Is for Baby Boomers," The News Wheel, March 13, 2018, https://thenewswheel.com/photos -jim-belushi-wants-you-to-know-that-the-2019-ford-transit -connect-wagon-is-for-baby-boomers/.

12. "FTX Super Bowl Don't Miss Out with Larry David," The World's Best Ads, YouTube video, February 14, 2022, https://www .youtube.com/watch?v=hWMnbJJpeZc.

13. "Rapunzel and Dunkin' at Home Coffee Commercial," Dunkin' at Home, YouTube video, October 1, 2021, https://www.youtube .com/watch?v=zHB3Hy7ophQ.

14. Lauroa Forman, "Sorry, Honey, It's Not You, It's Travel," *Wall Street Journal*, March 19, 2021, https://www.wsj.com/articles /sorry-honey-its-not-you-its-travel-11616157000.

15. "Oatly's Philadelphia-invented Cream Cheese Pre-launches Exclusively in Philadelphia, Home of the Company's Philadelphia-based R&D Lab," Oatly, February 22, 2023, https://www.oatly.com/en-us/things-we-do/brainwashing /cream-cheese-announcement.

16. "Say Hello to the Zoomsie™, the World's First Integrated Work-from-Home Fashion Solution," Cision, April 1, 2021, https:// www.prnewswire.com/news-releases/say-hello-to-the-zoomsie -the-worlds-first-integrated-work-from-home-fashion-solution -301260719.html.

17. Laura McQuarrie, "Professional Workwear Onesies," Trendhunter, April 3, 2021, https://www.trendhunter.com/trends /zoomsie.

18. Boris Ewenstein, Wesley Smith, and Ashvin Sologar, "Changing Change Management."

19. "RF Summit 2022," Ruder Finn, YouTube Video, October 18, 2022, https://www.youtube.com/watch?v=nIvc_Lz9jys.

20. Christopher Robert, Timothy C. Dunne, and Joyce Iun, "The Impact of Leader Humor on Subordinate Job Satisfaction: The Crucial Role of Leader–Subordinate Relationship Quality," *Group & Organization Management* 41, no. 3 (2016), 375–406, https:// doi.org/10.1177/1059601115598719.

21. "Table 16. Annual Average Job Openings Rates by Industry and Region, Not Seasonally Adjusted," US Bureau of Labor Statistics,

last modified March 8, 2023, https://www.bls.gov/news.release
/jolts.t16.htm.

5: Stand-Up Comedy

1. Joel Stein, "Humor Is Serious Business," Stanford Business,
July 11, 2017, https://www.gsb.stanford.edu/insights/humor
-serious-business.
2. Josephine Chinying Lang and Chay Hoon Lee, "Workplace
Humor and Organizational Creativity," *International Journal of
Human Resource Management* 21, no. 1 (2010), 46–60, https://doi
.org/10.1080/09585190903466855.
3. John Antonakis, Marika Finley, and Sue Liechti, "Can Charisma
Be Taught: Tests of Two Interventions," *Academy of Management
Learning & Education*, in press, https://serval.unil.ch/resource
/serval:BIB_FDC9DF7BA052.P001/REF.
4. "Gary Gulman: The Great Depresh (2019), Basketball (Clip),
HBO," HBO, YouTube video, October 3, 2019, https://youtu.be
/bM7CsJPFnYI.
5. "Bonnie McFarlane—Burning Down the House—This Is Not
Happening - Uncensored," Comedy Central, YouTube video,
March 14, 2017, https://www.youtube.com/watch?v=zKda9WY
_uxw&list=PLD7nPL1U-R5qsyLTu7bJsMNX5mbgbWlN8
&index=11.

6: Improvisational Comedy

1. "Whose Line—Stand Sit and Lie: Giving Birth," You-
Tube video, October 29, 2009, https://www.youtube.com
/watch?v=MTch-eHdqtU&list=PLhCHekcDVuQH9JXfrlFch3
-ABB_bz4YQu&index=5.
2. "Improv," Peppercomm, YouTube video, October 25, 2021,
https://www.youtube.com/watch?v=_s-if23kYgM.
3. "Improv Tip: Let Positivity Be Your Default," Scotty Watson Improv., n.d., https://www.scottywatsonimprov.com
/single-post/2018/07/28/scottys-improv-tip-4-let-positivity-be
-your-default.
4. "Maddy Got the Moves to Make You Wanna Move Out 😄
#WildNOut #shorts," YouTube video, February 25, 2023,
https://www.youtube.com/shorts/UQN3IjI6m_U.

5. Arpan Bhattacharyya, "Listening: The Most Important Skill That Nobody Teaches," Big Think, August 29, 2016, https://bigthink.com/high-culture/important-lessons-from-improv-on-listening/.

7: Sketch Comedy

1. Maggie Scudder, "How to Write a Comedy Sketch," Gold Comedy, February 25, 2022, https://goldcomedy.com/resources/how-to-write-a-comedy-sketch/.
2. "Fire Marshall Bill School Visit," The Time Traveler's Hangout, YouTube video, March 22, 2011, https://www.youtube.com/watch?v=_UpZZGeOP2Q.
3. "Substitute Teacher—Key & Peele," Comedy Central, YouTube video, October 17, 2012, https://www.youtube.com/watch?v=Dd7FixvoKBw.
4. Giovanni Sabato, "What's So Funny? The Science of Why We Laugh," *Scientific American*, June 26, 2019, https://www.scientificamerican.com/article/whats-so-funny-the-science-of-why-we-laugh/.
5. "The Kids in the Hall—Work Pig," *The Kids in the Hall*, YouTube video, June 6, 2021, https://www.youtube.com/watch?v=HX-6OjguJMU.
6. "Funny New Comedy—SNL," *Saturday Night Live*, YouTube video, February 20, 2017, https://www.youtube.com/watch?v=AMpRJwP5y9Q.
7. "'Weird Al' Yankovic—Eat It (Official 4K Video)," alyankovic, YouTube video, July 27, 2010, https://www.youtube.com/watch?v=ZcJjMnHoIBI.
8. "Unfrozen Caveman Lawyer—SNL," *Saturday Night Live*, YouTube video, August 3, 2019, https://www.youtube.com/watch?v=2AzAFqrxfeY.
9. "Office Boss with Cameron Diaz—SNL," *Saturday Night Live*, November 23, 2014, YouTube video, https://www.youtube.com/watch?v=OMJ-39TwHVE.
10. "Homie Da Clown—'Carnival,'" TheVernosius, YouTube video, July 6, 2009, https://www.youtube.com/watch?v=jpLF76iT790.
11. "Charlie Murphy's True Hollywood Stories: Rick James—Chappelle's Show," Comedy Central, YouTube video, November 25, 2019, https://www.youtube.com/watch?v=ry2XlLKctiI.

12. "Put a Bird on It! *Portlandia*, IFC," IFC, YouTube video, December 1, 2017, https://www.youtube.com/watch?v=GNpIOlD higw.

13. "Spartan Cheerleaders at Tryouts—SNL," *Saturday Night Live*, YouTube video, September 16, 2013, https://www.youtube.com/watch?v=SErOdLSlpkE.

14. "Mister Robinson's Neighborhood: Nutrition—*SNL*," *Saturday Night Live*, YouTube video, November 16, 2017, https://www.youtube.com/watch?v=K_MDCH-W2WU.

15. "Inside Amy Schumer—Size 12 (ft. Lena Dunham)," Comedy Central, YouTube video, May 18, 2016, https://www.youtube.com/watch?v=tw7xu2pZePw.

16. "Portlandia—Season 3—Candace's Son Visits the Feminist Bookstore," modestlyneutral, YouTube video, January 17, 2013, https://www.youtube.com/watch?v=e9r2o5ZnSHo.

8: Stand-Up Comedy in Business

1. Judah Schiller, "Average Human Attention Span by Age: 31 Statistics," The Treetop Therapy, April 18, 2023, https://www.thetreetop.com/statistics/average-human-attention-span.

2. "Thank You, Mr. President—The Press Conferences of JFK," President John Fitzgerald Kennedy, YouTube video, March 10, 2013, https://www.youtube.com/watch?v=sESlUEcfSxM.

3. "Steve Jobs Introducing the iPhone at MacWorld 2007," superapple4ever, YouTube video, December 2, 2010, https://www.youtube.com/watch?v=x7qPAY9JqE4.

4. "Elizabeth Holmes real voice vs fake voice," Scandalcast, YouTube video, May 18, 2022, https://www.youtube.com/watch?v=ymXePUOTnOs.

5. "CEO Patrick Collison's Email to Stripe Employees," Stripe, November 3, 2022, https://stripe.com/newsroom/news/ceo-patrick-collisons-email-to-stripe-employees.

6. Kathy Bloomgarden profile, LinkedIn, https://www.linkedin.com/in/kathy-bloomgarden-ab22369/.

7. Kali Hays, "Elon Musk Fired Dozens More Twitter Staff the Night Before Thanksgiving—Days After Saying He Was Done with Layoffs," *Business Insider*, November 24, 2022, https://www.businessinsider.com/elon-musk-fires-dozens-more-twitter-staff-night-before-thanksgiving-2022-11.

8. Chloe Berger, "No More Free Coffee and Layoff Warnings—Goldman Sachs Workers Experience a Rude Awakening," Yahoo! News, January 5, 2023, https://news.yahoo.com/no-more-free-coffee-layoff-192907988.html.

9. Bill Snyder, "Netflix Founder Reed Hastings: Make as Few Decisions as Possible," Stanford Business, November 3, 2014, https://www.gsb.stanford.edu/insights/netflix-founder-reed-hastings-make-few-decisions-possible.

10. "Laughter," *Psychology Today*, n.d., https://www.psychologytoday.com/us/basics/laughter.

11. Emilia Bunea, "Can Humor Make You a Better Leader?" *Psychology Today*, November 2022.

12. "D. B. Cooper Hijacking," FBI history, n.d., https://www.fbi.gov/history/famous-cases/db-cooper-hijacking.

13. Jessica Mesmer-Magnus, David J. Glew, and Chockalingam Viswesvaran, "A Meta-analysis of Positive Humor in the Workplace," *Journal of Managerial Psychology* 27 no. 2 (2012), 155–190, https://doi.org/10.1108/02683941211199554.

14. Brad Bitterly and Alison Wood Brooks, "Sarcasm, Self-Deprecation, and Inside Jokes: A User's Guide to Humor at Work," *Harvard Business Review*, July–August, 2020, https://hbr.org/2020/07/sarcasm-self-deprecation-and-inside-jokes-a-users-guide-to-humor-at-work.

15. Stacey Jones, "Let's Go Boldly into the Metaverse," *Marketing Insider*, August 17, 2022, https://www.mediapost.com/publications/article/376755/lets-go-boldly-into-the-metaverse.html.

16. Katie McCall, "What You Can Learn from Wendy's Social Media Strategy," Rival IQ, February 12, 2022, https://www.rivaliq.com/blog/wendys-social-media-strategy/.

17. "ALS Ice Bucket Challenge Compilation," *Toronto Star*, YouTube video, August 20, 2014, https://www.youtube.com/watch?v=44wcFkKylGw.

9: Improvisational Comedy in Business

1. Marc Baizman, "5 Principles of Improv Theater for Salesforce Admins," Salesforce, January 13, 2020, https://admin.salesforce.com/blog/2020/5-principles-of-improv-theater-for-salesforce-admins.

2. "The Heards and the Heard-Nots," Workforce Institute, 2021, https://workforceinstitute.org/wp-content/uploads/The-Heard -and-the-Heard-Nots.pdf.
3. Ralph G. Nichols and Leonard A. Stevens, "Listening to People," *Harvard Business Review*, September 1957, https://hbr .org/1957/09/listening-to-people.

10: Sketch Comedy in Business

1. Ben Franklin, *Poor Richard's Almanack*, 1753.
2. Greg Salmon, "5 Ways CEOs Can Improve Their Story-telling," *Forbes*, November 15, 2022, https://www.forbes .com/sites/forbesagencycouncil/2022/11/15/5-ways-ceos-can -improve-their-storytelling/?sh=f31548a2b2d8.
3. "PwC's 26th Annual Global CEO Survey," PWC, 2023, https:// www.pwc.com/gx/en/issues/c-suite-insights/ceo-survey-2023 .html.
4. "Peppercomm Attack Ad," Peppercomm, YouTube video, October 2, 2008, https://www.youtube.com/watch?v=C _SmkKDtPkA.
5. "Innovation SABRE Awards North America 2023 Finalists," Provoke Media, 2023, https://www.provokemedia.com/events -awards/sabre-awards/in2-sabre-awards/2023-in2-sabre-finalists.
6. Cathy Areu, "Cathy Areu: Thanks, Peloton! Nothing Says Merry Christmas Like Body-Shaming Your Wife," Fox News, December 4, 2019, https://www.foxnews.com/opinion/cathy-areu-peloton -christmas-gift-no-woman-wants.
7. Paddy Clarke, "Twitter Is Deeply Concerned for the Woman in the Peloton Christmas Commercial," Diply, updated September 4, 2021, https://diply.com/103172/twitter-is-deeply-concerned -for-the-woman-in-the-peloton-christ.
8. "TJMaxx Peppercomm The Dating Game Sketch," PepSquad, YouTube video, January 20, 2023, https://www.youtube.com /watch?v=NtVEqdsb9wc.
9. "Peppercomm's FIFTEEN Movie Trailer," Peppercomm, You-Tube video, December 9, 2010, https://www.youtube.com /watch?v=2sXWzI_aHnk.
10. "An Investigative Journalist's 'Inside' Look at Peppercomm," Peppercomm, YouTube video, October 22, 2009, https://www .youtube.com/watch?v=AVTq_3AAFxg.

11. Alison Griswold, "Here's Why Eliminating Titles and Managers at Zappos Probably Won't Work," *Business Insider*, January 6, 2014, https://www.businessinsider.com/zappos-holacracy-unlikely-to-work-2014-1.
12. "Chaos Reigns at Zappos as Company Moves Toward Self-Organization. Muuuwwaahaahaa :)," Zappos Insights, 2016, https://vimeo.com/139618687.
13. Philip Rucker, "Mitt Romney's Dog-on-the-Car-Roof Story Still Proves to Be His Critics' Best Friend," *Washington Post*, March 14, 2012, https://www.washingtonpost.com/politics/mitt-romneys-dog-on-the-car-roof-story-still-proves-to-be-his-critics-best-friend/2012/03/14/gIQAp2LxCS_story.html.

11: Bottom-Line Results

1. "World's Most Admired Companies," *Fortune*, https://fortune.com/ranking/worlds-most-admired-companies/.
2. "Fear Public Speaking More Than Death? Fear Not—The Audience Only Sees 20% of Your Nerves," Love Public Speaking, February 1, 2022, https://lovepublicspeaking.org/fear-public-speaking-more-than-death-fear-not-the-audience-only-sees-20-of-your-nerves.

INDEX

Index

peptides, brain, 19
A Perfect Match, 182
pitfalls, 63–64
Plaza, Aubrey, 131
point of view, 111, 192
Portlandia, 109, 111
Portman, Natalie, 73
Positivity Rule, 90–91, 162–63
post-visit survey results, 166
premise, 110, 191–92
presentation skills, 148, 195
Presto (Rush), 77
PricewaterhouseCoopers (PwC), 178
psychological safety, 33
punch lines, 73–75, 141–43
purpose-driven organizations,
    196–97
put-down comedy, 69–72, 138–41
PwC (PricewaterhouseCoopers),
    178

recruitment and retention, of
    employees, 44–48, 193–94
Regan, Brian, 58
relatability, 107, 181–84
RepMan blog, 191–92
Retire Your Risk, 153
RF (Ruder Finn), 51, 120–21
Richards, Michael, 63
Rivers, Joan, 69
Robert the Younger, 146
Rock, Chris, 138
ROI tips from Steve
    on acting out, 143–45
    on active listening, 167–70
    on "Below 44" campaign,
        154–55
    on board meetings, 25–26
    on "cattle call" meetings,
        126–27

on COVID-19 pandemic, 40–41
on emotional fullness, 120–21,
    123
on General Electric, 177–78
on improvisational comedy,
    92–93
on improvisational skills,
    159–60
on inversion, 186–87
on learning from failures, 131–34
on Oatly, 48–50
on put-down comedy, 139–41
on *RepMan* blog, 191–92
on stand-up debut, 12–13
on teamwork, 155–56
on "yes, and . . ." response,
    152–53
roll structure, 75–76
romantic relationships, 22–23
Ruder Finn, 51, 120–21
Rush, 77

Saint-Gobain, 177, 182
San Francisco Sketch Fest, 103
Saturday Night Live (SNL), 103
Schumer, Amy, 22, 39, 103
Seinfeld, 89, 159
self-assessment, 199–201
sensitivity, 63, 81, 126–28, 192
setups, 73–75, 141–43
The Shed 28, 22
short-form improvisation, 87–88,
    157–60
sketch comedy, 103–12
    forms of, 107–9
    key skills of, 104–7
    tools of, 109–11
sketch comedy in business, 175–92
    forms of, 184–90
    key skills of, 175–84

ABOUT THE AUTHORS

Steve Cody is the CEO of Peppercomm (www.peppercomm
.com), an award-winning strategic communications firm
headquartered in New York City.

Steve is immediate past chair of The Institute for Public
Relations (www.instituteforpr.org), a member of the nomi-
nating committee of The Page Society (www.page.org), and
serves on the advisory boards of the College of Charleston
and University of Florida, respectively.

Northeastern University has named him one of the
school's 100 most successful alumni. Steve coauthored the
2003 McGraw-Hill book *What's Keeping Your Customers Up
at Night?*

He is married with two children, two grandsons, and
a dog named Pippa. Steve describes himself as a climber,
a comedian, and a communicator (but not necessarily in
that order).

* * *

Clayton Fletcher is a professional comedian, actor, director,
public speaker, and musician. He is also an avid biker, avid
poker player, avid swimmer, and an avid user of the word
avid. Clayton has been featured on Hulu, Comedy Central,
CBS Sports Network, AXS-TV, Nick Mom, ESPN, MSNBC,
and Sirius/XM Radio. A regular at West Side Comedy Club,
Gotham Comedy Club, and New York Comedy Club, he has

toured with Jim Jefferies, David Alan Grier, Jessica Kirson, Gary Gulman, Norm Macdonald, and Cedric the Entertainer.

In the theater world, Clayton made his mark portraying dead singers such as Buddy Holly, Hank Williams, and Harry Chapin. Their stories weren't funny, so he turned to stand-up in 2003 and hasn't looked back since.

Clayton lives in Manhattan, where he has served as chief comedy officer at Peppercomm for more than fifteen years. He's on every social media platform @claytoncomic.